Your 7 Words
to a Happier You

YOUR 7 WORDS

TO A HAPPIER YOU

Unlock the Story Sabotaging Your Relationships

Jerry Giordano

BROWN BOOKS
PUBLISHING GROUP

Your 7 Words to a Happier You
Unlock the Story Sabotaging Your Relationships

Brown Books Publishing Group
Dallas, TX / New York, NY
www.BrownBooks.com
(972) 381-0009

A New Era in Publishing®

Publisher's Cataloging-In-Publication Data

Names: Giordano, Jerry, author.
Title: Your 7 words to a happier you : unlock the story sabotaging your relationships
    / Jerry Giordano.
Other titles: Your seven words to a happier you
Description: Dallas, TX ; New York, NY : Brown Books Publishing Group, [2024]
    | Includes bibliographical references.
Identifiers: ISBN: 978-1-61254-669-8 (hardcover) | LCCN: 2024930065
Subjects: LCSH: Happiness. | Self-realization. | Self-defeating behavior. | Self-
    esteem. | Interpersonal relations. | Mindfulness (Psychology) | Peace of
    mind. | LCGFT: Self-help publications. | BISAC: SELF-HELP / Personal
    Growth / Happiness. | SELF-HELP / Personal Growth / Self-Esteem.
Classification: LCC: BF575.H27 G56 2024 | DDC: 158.1--dc23

ISBN 978-1-61254-669-8
LCCN 2024930065

Printed in Canada
10 9 8 7 6 5 4 3 2 1

For more information or to contact the author, please go to
www.JerryGiordano.com.

*To my inner child, little jerry, whom I met
and ultimately set free during this journey.*

My last words to my mom were I love you.
*Her last words to me are now my final
words to you:* "I love you more."

The psychological rule says that when an inner situation is not made conscious, it happens outside, as fate.[1]
—**Carl Jung**

Translation: *Until you make the unconscious conscious, it will direct your life and you will call it fate.*

Once I discovered the unconscious 7 Word Story sabotaging my life, my decades of sleepwalking ended, and my conscious rebirth began.

Table of Contents

Preface

There is an old Buddhist proverb that states "Pain is inevitable. Suffering is optional." It's hard to imagine another quote as brilliantly simple and incredibly impactful—at least it seemed so in early 2017 when the world as I knew it came crashing down in front of me. Or rather, on top of me.

All my life, I'd prided myself on being resilient. I was an affable, seemingly unflappable dude from New Jersey who, despite what the name might imply, was not a tough guy by any means. Everyone I knew considered me an easygoing, roll-with-the-punches, doesn't-rock-the-boat kind of guy. In one word, you could say I was "likable." (Remember that description, if you will.) But from the time my mom died on January 18 until the breakup email from my girlfriend/ fiancée on the thirtieth, I wasn't able to feel much of anything besides numb. That weekend, my easygoing, roll-with-the-punches past caught up to me. Everything I had been holding in and suppressing for decades bum-rushed me all at once.

Pain, suffering, fear, anxiety—it all hit me along with two fully-fledged and equally terrifying panic attacks that were never on my bucket list. The first found me lying in a field of four-feet-tall grass and feeling initially like I was having a heart attack. I fell to my knees then dropped to my side. I couldn't breathe. All the pollen and snot covered me until all I could do was lie there unmoving, paralyzed. Seeing nothing but brown and green stems, I felt like a lost kid in a forest.

The second attack forced me under the dining room table on the cold, black concrete floor. It took everything I had to get air into my lungs. I was broken, depressed, and at the lowest point in my life. How low? Let's just say fracking could have been going on above me. All I wanted was to feel accepted, appreciated and acknowledged. Instead, what I felt was emptiness, desertion, and rejection. Sprinkle in a cup and a half of insignificant along with a pound or two of irrelevant, and you have Jerry giambotta (jom-boh-tah): a southern Italian everything stew I grew up eating in New Jersey. In short, I thought I was about to die.

All I kept thinking about was how my kids were going to come home from school and find me in a pool of my own phlegm. *Get on your feet*, I told myself. *Get the hell up. Come on, GET UP!* I could hear the words, but getting up even to my knees felt nothing short of impossible. For decades I had buried and deflected my feelings using humor as an avoidance tactic. I had relied instead on my master's degree in smart-ass and PhD in sarcasm in hopes the feelings would magically dissolve. This time, they didn't. They just festered and burrowed deeper inside me until the fear mutated into panic and paralysis. Even after the incident was over, I was unable to move. The splitting headache that remained was just an unpleasant reminder.

The not-so-funny thing about hitting rock bottom is this: You may be walking a tightrope, but it's actually lying flat on the ground. There's nowhere left to fall. So, as I saw it, I had two choices: lie face-planted in a twisted heap at the bottom of the deep, dark canyon or begin to dissect my unconscious habits and attempt to reduce the suffering as much as possible.

Fortunately for me, the process had already sort of begun. For two decades, I had attempted meditation. Unsuccessfully, I might add. I had somehow made up my mind that I wasn't good at meditation. That I couldn't do it and it was never going to happen for me. But something inside me was beginning to shift just a few months before my world caved in. I unmade my mind that I couldn't meditate and finally embraced it. Almost immediately, my newfound practice became a sanctuary for me. The universe had given me a three-month meditation runway leading up to my panic attacks and everything that followed.

I continued meditating two times a day. Most days it was more. Only now, uncontrollable tears often flowed within seconds of my meditation taking hold. My prized sanctuary became a raging river, flowing with decades of built-up sewage. Nothing could stop it, so I gave in to the process, and let everything flow.

Something in me had changed. I decided to feel everything for the first time in my life. And why not? Holding it all in and pretending that everything was OK, just fine, was not working. And I refused to go through another panic attack again. So, I let go emotionally, and the physical tears ran. This seemingly unstoppable tide extended into March. Then, after weeks of seemingly endless tears, they stopped. The pain of all that had occurred was still present, but the suffering had been washed away.

What had happened, as I understand it now, was the cathartic release of the utterly insane concept that I had control. Before this, the only thing I knew about depression and anxiety was that they were playing an endless game of tug-of-war in my life. I have since come to understand that depression comes from the attempt to control the past, and anxiety, from the attempt to control the future. I could do neither of those, but I knew I needed to feel differently about both my past and my future in order to get my life on a functional track. Though the uncovering of my 7 Word Story was still many miles down a dark, rutted road, I was on the right path at last.

Introduction

Relationship sabotage is an equal opportunity contentment killer for women and men. And when it comes to feelings, it seems both sexes learned early on to shove them down and keep those suckers at a distance. But why? Why do women and men keep hiding their feelings from each other even though many have been through or are still in therapy, have tried enlightenment seminars, have read shelves full of self-help books, and remind themselves daily to *think positive thoughts*? The answer is simple: we have a sabotaging story built into our unconscious. Your story may be different than mine, but the result is the same: it is sabotaging our relationship with ourselves, and in turn, our relationship with others.

Why do we do it? Because we're unaware. More specifically, our actions come from the overriding yet unconscious story we created at a very young age that continues to operate us whether we're in our teens, twenties, thirties, or our eighties. I know it because I was there.

In retrospect, my sabotaging behavior is now easy to explain. I was sleepwalking. No, not for a night or two. Not for a few weeks or even years, but for more decades than I care to recollect. If you had asked me during all the years I was struggling to "find myself" if I was conscious and in charge of my life, I would have bet anything that I was indeed the captain of my own ship. Good thing no bookies were nearby. It would have been an epic fail. I had an unconscious 7 Word Story running my life. It not only ran it, but sabotaged it—my relationships, my self-esteem, and ultimately, my *contentezza* ("contentment" in Italian).

My focus on contentment instead of happiness is intentional. Happiness is impossible to quantify. It's something that is constantly pursued, even chased, and yet, even if we *think* we've somehow corralled it, it slips away as quickly as it appears. Turns out happiness is that fleeting moment that occurs the instant before we need more happiness. Everywhere around us, we're being sold a bill of goods that happiness is just one exchange, one destination, one purchase, one click or positive thought away. We've become addicted to searching for and potentially owning that elusive outcome. The unintended consequence of our ongoing pursuit of happiness turns out to be contradictory: more unhappiness.

Contentment, on the other hand, is serenity. Contentment is ease and acceptance. Not a thing to own but a place to be. Sitting in satisfaction and gratitude for where we are. Unencumbered fulfillment.

Uncovering my unconscious story changed everything for me, and I'm here to help you do the same—to discover the story unconsciously driving your cycle of unhappiness. And just as importantly, get you to realize it's within your power to fix it. Your *contentezza*.

Hi, my name is Jerry. I am a contentment counselor, dot connector, and recovering sleepwalker.

I've spent much of my professional life in advertising, marketing, and branding in NYC, Chicago, Los Angeles, Austin and Dallas. A copywriter and creative director, I have been labeled somewhat of a "creative" guy. A moniker bestowed on people who conceive, envision, and imagine stuff for a living. My job has been to create ideas that people have not seen and can relate to on a personal and emotional level. My days are spent observing, scratching, scraping, and digging for those dots that connect us all. I became quite skilled at collecting, inspecting and connecting dots.

I see the world as a bunch of links, points, ideas, concepts, thoughts, philosophies, or loose ends looking to attach one to another. Connecting begins with collecting. The aggregating and accumulation of pieces: things, ideas, concepts, and sometimes, seemingly useless facts. Information that appears as a dot may lead to another and another. Especially when it relates to the human psyche or behavior, collecting leads to inspecting. Alone, most dots aren't very developed or relevant. But woven together, the tapestry becomes apparent.

Mark Twain put it in perspective: "All ideas are secondhand, consciously and unconsciously drawn from a million outside sources." When we have an experience, we drop a dot. Have another, drop another dot. This occurs each time we learn something new, whether it becomes a perceived failure or apparent success.

In many ways, this book is about connections joined together from events, observations, feelings, facts, and countless hours of introspection in the form of meditation. Though these first dots that built the concept are from my own life, it will get you to think about your dots as well.

Before and during the writing of this book, I interviewed over two hundred men and women—the youngest participant was thirteen years old and the oldest was ninety-four, and the rest spanned just about every age in between—many of whom I've had multiple follow-up conversations with. You'll get to meet some of them in Part II. The goal of the initial interviews was to uncover the person's 7 Word Story—which is the whole concept this book is shaped around. This also gave me insights and a better understanding of why they do what they do. Why they, as I did for decades, unknowingly sabotaged their relationships with others, but not before sabotaging the one with themselves first.

Who we "are" in our society is often misguidedly based on what we do. We are too often labeled either by ourselves, family, or society by what job we occupy. For instance, the people I have spent time with and interviewed extensively for this book "do" a lot of things for a living, but that's not who they "are." I've uncovered the 7 Word Stories of teachers, lawyers, engineers, stay-at-home moms and dads, students, artists, contractors, paralegals, designers, photographers, woodworkers, insurance investigators, makeup artists, physical therapists, social workers, programmers, a psychic, marketing executives, a housekeeper, a dog trainer, nurses, bankers, a female bounty hunter, a HR director, a doctor, a hairdresser, a psychologist, and a welder. Just about everyone except a politician.

But all these professions mentioned are *labels*. They represent what people do for a living but not *who* they are. They, you, and me are, first and foremost, people. We are not humans having a spiritual experience but spiritual beings having a human one. My belief is that the spiritual part of us doesn't give a flying fig-stuffed tart about what we do for a job, but instead cares about what we're doing while we're on this planet. What I did for a living was advertising, marketing, and branding, but what I was doing was, in fact, sleepwalking. Until, that is, I connected the dots that changed my relationships with everyone. Especially myself.

I Found Myself in a Giant Hole. Then I Stopped Digging.

This book is about my discovery and the step-by-step process I've found that uncovers the unconscious, game-changing 7 Words that bring about peace, contentment, and freedom. It'll help you find the answer to why you do the things you do—not humanity or a group of people, but specifically you. This is not a catchall system or a generic self-help book. It's a book unlike any I've read, and trust me, I've read dozens of them. If any of the books I devoured over the decades or all the *positive thinking*, *manifesting* and *visualization* had worked, there would have been no reason to discover my 7 Word Story and ultimately write this book.

Why didn't any of them work? Because self-esteem, well-being, and contentment are emotional right-brain issues. The 7 Word Story is an emotion-based story we created at a young age that can't be resolved or even understood with left-brain logic and explanations. Magical solutions such as *love yourself, believe you're perfect just as you are, think positive thoughts*, or *change how you think* just don't work. They're an outside logical mentality that has no connection with what your unconscious emotional brain is feeling. This disconnect is what keeps you in a perpetual state of unfulfillment. Uncovering your emotional *why* story is what sets us free.

Searching for that "logical" solution had me on a perpetual merry-go-round for decades, and I'm convinced I would still be on it if my journey from the ashes hadn't led to that all-important *why*. By uncovering and understanding my why, I am now able to help you find yours.

This book is broken down into three major sections, each with a different focus.

Part I: My 7 Words gives you the background that prompted my discovery. It takes you through the roughest months of my life. It'll show you the power of meditation and how it helped me reset my ego enough to uncover this process. All the observations, connections, transformations, and interpretations regarding this unearthing happened for better or for worse in a vacuum. The process was illogical and nonlinear, as are most right-brain discoveries. It took trust in my meditative connection to the emotional powers of the universe to connect those dots.

Part II: Their 7 Words shares the universal findings of everyone who has done Their 7 Words. Here, you get to meet some of them, hear how their unconscious words have affected their lives, and how those words have sabotaged their relationships in the past.

Part III: Your 7 Words are all about you and filling in your own words so that you can find the *why* you do what you do. You'll learn why you habitually say "sorry" all the time. Why you might be a people-pleaser or know folks who are, and why perpetual people-pleasing has become such an epidemic. Why you felt the way you did growing up and why those feelings persist. We'll uncover your two main words that drive your personality and lead to your sabotaging ways. And finally, I'll show you how to shed all those sabotaging ways and leave you with something more rewarding: self-acceptance.

In the simplest of terms, we're all in search of the same things. Appreciation. Acceptance. And being loved. Emotional results that can't come from logical, left-brained efforts. In this book, we will uncover your secret right-brain *why* you don't feel appreciated, satisfied, understood, listened to, or respected across all the relationships in your life, especially the one with yourself. More self-discovery than self-help, uncovering My 7 Words dissipated my negative, habitual overthinking and unearthed my previously nonexistent self-esteem. It also brought back the innocence and simplicity I lost in childhood. It is my hope that by the end of these pages, it will also change how you look at yourself, your relationships, and your life.

PART I

My 7 Words

1

The Crashing

Jen was the person I wanted to spend the rest of my life with—the one I'd been waiting my entire lifetime for. The person who got me more than all others combined. She was loving, caring, and giving. She was incredibly affectionate, which was something that had previously seemed unattainable. With her, it finally dawned on me what all the unrelatable people writing love poems and love songs were waxing poetic about.

There's a famous line from the movie *Jerry Maguire*: "You had me at hello." That wasn't us. The moment that red door opened for the first time, no words were necessary. The day we met, we talked, swam, flirted, laughed, and talked more. We smiled when we caught the other sneaking a subtle glance across the pool. The very next day we became exclusive. The connection grew and matured. The desire and intimacy kept topping itself, year after passionate year. We even coined the appropriate name for it: Hot Monogamy. We weren't without cute nicknames either. Because we were to be "together forever" and penguins mated for life, she became "Penny" for penguin, and I was "Tux," as in the usual penguin attire. We had never done the nickname thing in other relationships, but we'd never been with anyone like each other before. So, Penny and Tux it was. Nothing out there could top this.

But exactly one week before Christmas in 2016, I discovered my tuxedo was a rental.

We had just finished making love as we did nearly every night we were together when she rolled over and kissed me goodnight. Then, as nonchalantly as whispering, "Sweet dreams, honey," she blurted out, "We're not going to be together for Christmas and New Year's like we planned. Christmas day I'm flying to Belize to figure out if we're going to be together anymore."

It felt like someone smashed my temple with a brick.

"By yourself?" I asked.

"Yes."

No previous discussion about being unhappy, seeing other people, or breaking up. Just that baffling, blindsiding, bewildering Belize bomb. Right then, the life I'd pictured for decades to come began fading away like images in an old photo album. The one person who got me, whom I trusted more than everyone else I ever knew put together, just flipped my world like a bubbling pancake on a hot griddle.

The next morning, both of us acted as if nothing had happened. Same with the rest of the week. We made love every night and spent all of Christmas Eve with her kids and her parents. Christmas morning, I drove her to the airport, and we kissed goodbye at the curb. It was the most emotional she had been in our four-and-a-half years together. She walked toward the sliding doors and instead of dropping her bags and running back into my arms like in the movies, the doors slowly closed behind her. She was off to Belize.

Home for the Holidaze

My kids were skiing with my ex-wife, so I spent Christmas at the movies chomping on popcorn and chewing up time. My ceaseless thoughts and runaway mind were all I had. So, I booked a last-minute ticket to New Jersey for the next morning and after an exhausting day of planes, trains and Ubermobiles, I surprised my mom and dad late on the evening of the twenty-sixth. My mom greeted me with, "Oh look who's here," followed by, "You need a haircut." All was right with the world.

The next day my mother had a doctor's appointment. What we thought was a normal doctor's visit turned out to be anything but. As bluntly and with as little bedside manner I had witnessed since Jen nine days earlier, Dr. Ice-for-Veins told us there was nothing she could do for her, and we needed to take my mom home to hospice. My brain understood what hospice meant, but my emotions were completely without reference. How does one process hearing their mom's previous birthday and Christmas two days earlier would be her last? My eyes darted from doctor to Dad to Mom and back, searching for some clue how to react. All three of them sat like stone monuments. The doctor never said why Mom was going home to die. And we didn't ask. I've never felt so helpless before or since.

After a night in the hospital, the next day we set her up with home hospice care. It all was happening so quickly and Jen's soothing voice was the only one I wanted to hear. But she was somewhere in Belize—a country whose name, when translated, is Mayan for "muddy-watered." The irony was not lost on me.

I spent that week at my mom's side then flew back to Texas on New Year's Day. When the fiancée returned, she was nothing but kind, sweet, and understanding. All the traits that had attracted me to her from day one. Other than asking her, "How was your trip?" and her responding, "Nice," there was no mention of Belize or what she was thinking. In fact, it was as if nothing had happened.

On January 18, I called my mom to check in and see how she was doing. She was tired and I told her I would call back tomorrow. Before we hung up, I told her I loved her. She responded with something she'd never said before: "I love you more!"

That night, three weeks after my mom went into hospice, she passed away.

I told Jen the news and she was incredibly thoughtful, loving, and compassionate. She was especially moved by my mom's last words, telling me how touching that was as she fell asleep on my chest.

Morning arrived and I was getting ready to fly back to New Jersey again. While showering, the steamy door opened, and Jen slid in. She was extremely playful. Mischievous. Engaging. Morphing into a flirtatious, kittenlike tease. On my end, all too familiar desire. Comfort. Connection. There was nothing else I would have rather been doing than spend the morning in the shower with her. *My Uber will be here in twenty minutes* was my reluctant response to her invitation. "I guess you'll have to wait until you get back" was her enticing response. I needed a cold shower after my shower.

Dressed and waiting for my driver, we had a long, impassioned kiss by the front door. Softly I whispered, "I love you." She responded immediately with "I love you more."

I pulled away quickly. "That's not a joke. You know how much that means to me."

"I know. I wasn't joking," she said and kissed me again.

I was off to bury my mom, and Jen couldn't have handled things any better. Perfect words. Perfect sentiment. Perfect consoling by someone you love. And who loves you more.

We spoke every day I was gone. And not only did everything seem fine, but her words were so extremely comforting and supportive that my love for her kept topping itself—which made the following discovery even more confusing.

When I returned from New Jersey to pick up my car and go see my kids, the back seat and floor were haphazardly filled with my clothes, shoes, and miscellaneous items. Did I miss a text or call while I was busy burying my mom and consoling my dad? Where did this come from? This kind of behavior was so out of character from the person I had fallen madly in love with. I fell in love with the way she treated my scars and insecurities with such tenderness, love, and care. Now she was my primary gaping open wound.

Not wanting to even hear her voice at that point, I sent a text: *After my mom's death and my honesty, vulnerability, and openness with you this week, it hurt me incredibly to see my stuff tossed in the back seat with no warning or explanation.* She apologized, saying, "I'm sorry if I hurt you. It was insensitive and poorly timed." My response was *Not if you hurt me, you did hurt me.* She answered with "Yes, good clarification. That, not if." It had become apparent that the woman who prided herself on her "communication" skills, who had all the answers when it came to self-awareness and whose favorite word from her multiple "Personal Development" weekends was *integrity*, had jumped the shark. This led to a text from me that said: *I have no idea. No clue what you want from me or from us. The damn goal keeps moving . . .*

I received this two-line email the following morning: "There is no we or us for me to be in or be like anymore. That's the problem with emails, hard to convey tone and I don't want to give a mixed message."

And that is how she decided to end our four-and-a-half-year relationship. A few days later, I went to her place to pick up the rest of my things. Mostly shirts, a few suits and whatever was left she hadn't already "packed" for me. The two most important things for me to retrieve were her engagement ring and the authentic INTERSTATE 35 highway sign. It was how I proposed to her—three-inch adhesive black letters on the back of the four-square-feet road sign that said: MARRY ME? I-35 is the highway that runs through Austin and Dallas, and I had proposed to her at exactly the halfway point between our homes on a bridge over the Brazos River in Waco, Texas. I removed the heavy metal sign from her kitchen wall and placed it on top of my clothes in the back seat. No time to scrape off the MARRY ME? on the back. That would have to wait.

While loading my car on pick-up-your-junk day, I asked why we still made love every night we were together like nothing whatsoever was wrong even though she was obviously planning on ending our relationship. Her response was surprisingly simple: "Why should our sex life suffer because we're going through what we're going through?" What was left of my mind was now blown. Right then, her prized word, *integrity*, was in a galaxy far, far away. While everything in my outside world was crumbling, my internal universe began to fold in on itself like a black hole.

As I backed out of the garage, I watched her slowly disappear as the door sank to meet the driveway. No final words. No *Better Call Saul* Jimmy and Kim farewell hand gestures. Nothing.

In my favorite "documentary" about my home state of New Jersey, *The Sopranos*, Janice Soprano's therapist coaches her to break up with Ralphie gently: "Move from the darkness and towards the light. Speak the truth, but with the compassion and respect that you're famous for." Janice broke up with Ralph Cifaretto by kicking him down a flight of stairs for not taking his shoes off in the house. Previously, she ended her engagement with Richie Aprile by shooting him twice in the chest at the dinner table. Maybe I'd gotten off lucky. Although at that moment, my heart felt like the aforementioned Richie's ticker. Full of holes.

That is how I started the first month of 2017. My life had gone from a Capra film to a Hitchcock retrospective in just a few weeks. In hindsight, all this was a precursor to my ultimate awakening from decades of sleepwalking. Unfortunately, hindsight was a long way away.

My Cup Runneth Over

Now, there was one more woman in my life at the time: my ex-wife. We were renegotiating our divorce decree, dealing with my lawyers, her lawyers, and unfortunately, her, when absolutely necessary. We both had 50 percent custody of our kids. I was spending half of my time in Dallas working with clients, half my time in Austin with my kids, and the other half driving the four hours each way once or twice a week. I had been juggling six and seven balls, only to drop five of them, sometimes six. During our separation and divorce we were doing something called "nesting" where our kids stayed in the house and we would leave when the other was with the kiddos. Every Monday and Tuesday night was my time with the kids; every Wednesday and Thursday was hers. Every other weekend we were on for five days. Some call it 5-2-2-5 custody. It was something we wanted to do for our kids. Nesting, I later discovered, was meant for months—maybe a year. We had been doing it for five-plus years by this point.

According to our initial divorce agreement, certain financial and housing issues were to be settled by spring of 2016. I agreed to put it off until May 2017 for the stability of our kids. And to avoid confrontation. I have no regrets, although it did add greatly to my stress, anxiety and ever-increasing dropped ball count. The new deadline was fast approaching and something needed to be settled in my life, and this was a good place to start. The good news was I believed I was already as low as I could possibly be. But then my life began to resemble the history of Russia, summarized in five words . . . AND THEN IT GETS WORSE.

Finding myself completely out of capacity and inside a dark situational depression, the only place I felt any semblance of peace or structure was in my meditation practice. But even that had taken an unexpected turn. Instead of the usual calm, now, seconds into my meditation, tears came uncontrollably pouring out. The giant, soggy outbursts were unstoppable. Sometimes, meditation wasn't even necessary for the deluge. During these first few months of 2017, all the tears, pain, and anguish I had suppressed my entire life came rushing through my red, swollen eyes, gushing uncontrollably. Tropical storm Jerry had arrived.

I found myself in a strange new place—ROCK BOTTOM. POPULATION 001. I not only felt more alone than I ever imagined possible, but I also felt drained. And soggy.

Rock Bottom Has a Silver Lining

We've all heard of post-traumatic stress disorder (PTSD), the clinical term for a diagnosed mental-health condition triggered by a painful, stressful, or traumatic event. It can be debilitating and last weeks, months, or years if not diagnosed and treated. There is also something called post-traumatic growth (PTG): advancement or growth from a traumatic incident. In other words, the proverbial silver lining inside that dark, nebulous mess. PTG can also be called "benefit finding." It describes creating a positive psychological outcome despite adversity and while dealing with challenging events.

Viktor E. Frankl's *Man's Search for Meaning* encapsulates this kind of remarkable growth. I read the book a year or so before I face-planted and before I'd started my meditative practice, not knowing at the time how relevant it would be to my life. Frankl believed that it was possible to use suffering as a way to find a sense of purpose in life and go on to achieve great things. A neurologist, psychiatrist, philosopher and author, Frankl found himself a Jewish prisoner of Nazi Germany. He spent more than three years inside two of the most notorious concentration camps imaginable: Auschwitz and Dachau.

Frankl wrote the following in 1946, less than a year after he was liberated from the Dachau concentration camp:

> If there is a meaning in life at all, then there must be a meaning in suffering. Suffering is an ineradicable

part of life, even as fate and death. Without suffering and death human life cannot be complete.

The way in which a man accepts his fate and all the suffering it entails, the way in which he takes up his cross, gives him ample opportunity—even under the most difficult circumstances—to add a deeper meaning to his life. It may remain brave, dignified and unselfish. Or in the bitter fight for self-preservation he may forget his human dignity and become no more than an animal. Here lies the chance for a man either to make use of or to forgo the opportunities of attaining the moral values that a difficult situation may afford him. And this decides whether he is worthy of his sufferings or not . . . Such men are not only in concentration camps. Everywhere man is confronted with fate, with the chance of achieving something through his own suffering.[1]

Frankl was the creator of Logotherapy, which is considered the "third Viennese school of psychotherapy," with Sigmund Freud being the first, followed by Alfred Adler. Frankl's Logotherapy (the word coming from the Greek word *logos*, or "reason") is built around one very clear and simple concept: Meaning. That the most powerfully motivating force in a person's life is to find meaning in that life. Plain and simple. No matter what pain and suffering we endure— and few have seen and lived through more pain and suffering than Viktor Frankl—we have free will, the will to choose how we respond to stimulus. No matter what, we have the power to determine our attitude at any given moment, including and especially during times of pain and suffering.

I am not trying to use my pain, anguish, depression, or my rock bottom to one-up what anyone else has gone or is now going through, especially given what Viktor Frankl experienced and survived. But my pain was still real. It was what I was going through, and it was something I wanted, no, *needed*, to figure out because nothing in my life before ever came close to what I was now feeling.

Viktor's lifelong devotion to helping people bring meaning into their lives stuck with me. There were many thoughts and conversations with myself during these dank, dark days. According to all the research, we human types have sixty-two hundred thoughts per day. In retrospect, most of my sleepwalking gibberish, deliberations, and self-dialogue at the time was worthless trash. But the one reoccurring nugget was this thought: If Viktor Frankl could live through losing his wife, baby, mother, father, and brother at the hands of Hitler's Final Solution, then survive three years in concentration camps and go on to live a life not only worth living but inspirational, then there might be hope for me to somehow find my way.

Frankl's inspiration became a future dot to connect, and an inspirational one at that. My shattered heart didn't kill me. Nor did my depression, panic attacks, or the tsunami of endless tears. Sleepwalking through life as I was, the only thing I remember feeling was fear. Now, courtesy of already being at rock bottom with no place lower to fall, the fear had dissipated. What I was feeling for the first time was hurt, sadness, regret, disappointment and grief. My newfound "acceptance" of those other feelings came courtesy of Buddhism, which gifted me the words, "Pain is inevitable. Suffering is optional." My yet undiscovered wisdom and knowledge were wholly born of pain. Apparently, this sort of future understanding requires pain to activate. Now that the pain was firmly in place, it was time to figure out not only what caused me to face-plant into rock bottom, but why I felt broken and unworthy my entire life. And if there was some meaning to be found in all this, that would be an unexpected yet cherished bonus.

2

The "Make Me Be OK" Practices

Growing up I knew two things for certain. One, I needed fixing. Two, I had no idea how. It seemed to me everyone on TV was either strong, smart, attractive, happy or accomplished. Or all the above. To make matters worse, I thought I was the only person who felt I was none of the above.

We have created a society where everyone, including the people we perceive to be put together, is judging their insides by everyone else's outsides. Everywhere we look, we see these put-together people with their amazing put-together lives that make our own lives seem so not put together. Our "news" or "reality shows," Instagram, Facebook, TikTok, and other social media feeds are overflowing with stories and images that give us the illusion that the people we're looking at have it all: a great job, family, relationship, car, mansion, teeth, breasts, biceps—it's a never-ending list.

There's an old Hollywood saying that "movies are real life with all the boring parts left out." In our current world, social media is more words and pictures that make the everyday life of the person posting seem bigger, exciting, or more important than it is. And just like the movies that Hollywood creates, those social media worlds are also fantasyland. Intended to give the viewer a made-up image of perfection. The operative word being "image." We can also go with "made-up." Same difference.

Unconsciously (there's that word again), all these images and projections begin to chip away at our self-esteem and take their toll on us. We believe we're missing something, but we're not sure what. We keep looking. Searching. Trying to find "It"— whatever that is. We mistakenly believe we're the only ones who feel broken and unsatisfied. I understand all that because I was in that hole that kept me in perpetual outward comparison and inward judgmental mode.

But as Grandpa Giordano said, "Don't believe anything you hear and half of what you see." The people we see every day on the news and social media with their beautifully crafted and curated lives are as insecure or possibly more so than the rest of us onlookers. While we're judging our insides by their outside images, they're doing the same thing with the images of people that have it better than them. And there will always be someone thinner, richer, or who has more followers than they do. Hey Poppy G, time to raise that *don't believe what we see* number from 50 to maybe 90 percent.

To compensate for this feeling of lack, I was constantly and subconsciously running a con game with myself. Absurdly unaware that the persona I was projecting to the world was merely a smokescreen. Where I grew up in New Jersey, there is a common term for something that's a fake. It's not-so-lovingly referred to as a *fugazi* (*foogāzē*). If a situation or interaction is a sham or screwed up beyond belief, it's also a *fugazi*. I can honestly confess my life was indeed a *fugazi*. And worst of all, I had no idea whatsoever. In order to cover up my perpetual "not good enough" feeling, I defaulted to my alter *fugazi* ego: Likable Jerry.

The *what* was obvious—I felt broken. The bigger question was *why?*

Even in my teens, twenties and thirties, my thoughts about myself were second-rate at best. I was remarkably substandard in my mind when compared to the outside world. There was *me,* and there was *them.* Maybe by midlife that feeling of "not good enough" would magically rise to the surface, get scrubbed off, and slither down the drain during a morning shower. Even my unending search for meaning was unconscious. What exactly was my plan? Apparently it was just more, and more, and more self-help books. More fix-myself classes and courses. More therapy. Another weekend immersion seminar. Like being a man on a horse, galloping all day long, jumping fences, falling, and getting back on. It *seemed* as though I were on a mission. But if someone had stopped me and asked, *where are you going?* My answer would most likely have been, "I don't really know. Ask the horse."

Sure, it was all happening to me. I was there—physically present, anyhow. But aware? Not so much.

Self-Help Books

I was in my twenties when I picked up my first of many "self-help" books. It was titled, *I'm OK—You're OK* by Thomas Anthony Harris. The book was touted as a practical guide for solving life's problems. Well, it was the late 1970s, and "life's problems" were everywhere. The unemployment rate averaged 7.9 percent with some years exceeding 9 percent. By decade's end, a thirty-year mortgage had reached 11.2 percent. Crime was widespread. We had skyrocketing inflation, stagflation, and any *flation* imaginable. Lest we forget gas lines and the highest misery index since the Great Depression. Car theft was rampant—over 1.2 million cars were stolen . . . *in New York City alone!* The raw, gooey residue from the Vietnam War loitered over everything like a damp, woolen cloak. I hid under my own personal dark blanket by pulling my "Hi, I'm Jerry and I'm a happy-go-lucky guy" persona over my head. Everything at that time felt inescapable.

So, I read the book. Then reread it. All-in-all, I read *I'm OK—You're OK* five times. I still didn't feel OK. It just reinforced my thinking that everyone *but* me was just fine.

I'M OK was my first foray into the "fix yourself" world of self-help but certainly not my last. I spent decades in search of the illusive I'm OK moniker.

It seemed like the more self-help I devoured, the hollower I felt for not getting any better—a paradox not lost on me even at the time. I often thought these books made some great points but either I wasn't getting the big picture or maybe I was just too broken to ever get fixed. Or, just maybe, I hadn't found the right one. The one with all the magical answers. So I kept searching.

Radio Psychiatrists

My foray into Project Fix Myself actually began with hundreds of hours spent listening to call-in radio psychiatrist shows that saturated NYC radio stations at the time. One afternoon, I was driving to the beach, or as we call it in New Jersey, "Down the Shore." My radio was on AM from listening to the Yankees game the night before. There was a female psychiatrist with a strong yet soothing voice talking to regular people who called in with their problems. The whole concept seemed as foreign to me as self-esteem itself, but I was a fixer-upper, so maybe some of her wisdom could rub off on me. So, I listened. Found a few more call-in shows, and I was hooked. Many of the callers had some specific issues, and I imagine it was nice for them to have someone who would actually listen to them. It was in some ways soothing for me too, even though it was their problems being discussed. It never occurred to me back then but now, I do believe hearing someone care to listen to someone else's problems felt somehow soothing and loving to me as well. It was so foreign in my life that even the possibility of feeling secondhand interest was nice. It kept me listening. I was riveted to these shows for years, spurring my curiosity about the human psyche even more. I thought about calling in more than a few times, but I didn't really have a question other than "Why do I feel so empty?" I didn't want them to think that was an inane request. Within a year, I was face-to-face with a therapist of my very own. The decades-long pursuit of my big fix was now on.

Therapy

There were four unattached stints on couches in three different states. During my first therapy stretch, I recall being angry at my mom for teaching me to do my own laundry and requiring me to do it by myself at age nine. My therapist sided with me and chastised her. An ongoing theme in my personal therapy attempted to pinpoint a big emotional incident or ongoing issue from my childhood. Some neglect we could hang on to that was the turning point. There wasn't one. I tried for the longest time to make one of mom's actions or inactions be the big moment, but it seemed to be a waste of time. My parents weren't at all abusive. Or unkind. Just uncomplicated, overwhelmed, unemotional, and detached. I did have an internal reaction to all this. I convinced myself I didn't have horrible or cruel parents and my issues weren't their fault. I was the broken one. A thought I never could get myself to share with any therapist or anyone else.

Life-Coaches

I saw my first two life coaches while living in Los Angeles. One was recommended by a friend who was obsessed with climbing the corporate ladder and constantly raved about his guy. His "guy" was careful not to name-drop but did title-drop early and often. My second coach was excited to show me his new car and his massive koi pond that encircled his feng-shui-inspired home in the hills. I was impressed but not inspired. Both "coaches" were all about goals, objectives and outcomes and getting me to set and reach them all. One got me to do a "goal board" and the other a "dream board." These were to motivate me to make more money and be more powerful, and that would eventually cure my ills. My boards were filled with items that exemplified "success," in outward manifestations at least. Selling the two screenplays I had written by then, getting big Hollywood script deals and what those big checks from those big sales could get me and my family. My boards were good. Heck, I had been in advertising for a long time by then and I certainly knew how to make a kick-ass presentation. That wasn't the issue. It all just felt like a giant four-color cliché of what the dream of success was supposed to be like.

My last life coach was in Austin, Texas. A kind, fatherly figure who also focused on my career advancement but came the closest to understanding my internal strife. His "inspiration list" at least attempted to touch on internal stimuli, but the assignment also missed the mark with me just like the visual boards the other two had me make. He was big into manifesting. It didn't resonate at all.

I was searching for clarity and understanding of myself, and what I was getting from my life coaches was how to be more successful in my career. Reluctantly, I went along with the notion that if I had more success, money or fame, I would somehow understand what was broken inside me or I wouldn't care any longer and that feeling of *not enough* would somehow miraculously vanish. It didn't. They kept giving me left-brained solutions, trying to Logic me to joy, happiness, and self-acceptance. It was just like therapy but without the advanced degrees.

Seminars

I ended up doing a couple of intensive weekend seminars, which promised to "bring about positive, permanent shifts in the quality of your life" in just three days. These crash courses in self-rah-rah-rah were invigorating, promising, and as they like to say, life-changing. I prefer to not name the company, but if you've explored that sort of self-help, you will know them. They do seminars in 125 cities in 21 countries and, according to Wikipedia, have 500 employees and 7,500 volunteers. They have been accused of being cultlike, which didn't bother me and still doesn't. During the highly intensive weekend consisting of three 12-hour days, they find an "event" in your life that has caused deep-seated trauma. After many hours of "digging," I came up with an incident that happened between me (around age ten) and my mom where I got off a ride at an amusement park and I told her I was going throw up in public, and she screamed at me. That was my "significant" moment of truth. And that's what I ran with.

By the last night of camp, the eighty of us long-weekenders were armed with our newfound aha moment, excavated wisdom, and a new can-do group energy. The last few hours were more of a pep rally with people inviting friends and family to join in the celebration and recruit people for the next seminar. I remember wanting my story about my mom to be life-changing and become this turning point. I got home that Sunday night completely exhausted from thirty-six hours of bombardment. For the next few days, I tried to make sense of why that story was so life-changing for me. The reason I couldn't figure out why was because it wasn't. Once the group placebo effect wore off, I knew the issue wasn't my mom embarrassing me when I was a kid. It was with me. But I still didn't know why, so I kept on searching.

Hypnosis, Clairvoyants, Astrologers—Literally Anyone

Outings to psychics; astrologers; a past-life regression in Venice, California (where else?); an intuitive who reintroduced me to people from beyond; hypnosis; and courses from every self-help guru promising me the thing I was constantly seeking: the ever-elusive feeling of just *being friggin' OK.*

To that end, I once spent a sticky summer evening in the basement of a large old house in Newark, New Jersey, waiting for a four-foot-something elderly female Portuguese clairvoyant to impart her wisdom. I was dating a woman named JoAnn at the time; her brother-in-law, Al, who was of Portuguese descent, suggested we come with—so there we were.

The massive basement had a floor-to-ceiling altar with candles and statues. The men and I sat in wooden folding chairs on one side and JoAnn and the other women were on the flip side of the underground bunker. The stale, musty basement had a unique scent. Maybe it was the oils and the burning incense mixed with the "Jersey Juice"—the ninety-plus-percent summer humidity that gave it such a distinctive tang. It was like a Stephen King novel with a scratch and sniff cover.

Street noises and garbled alley scents drifted through the too-few basement windows in a desperate bid at circulation. They failed miserably. Talking wasn't allowed, and that magic time-killing machine known as the iPhone was decades away. Time slinked and skulked as slowly as the hulking summer air. Sometime after three a.m., I got a finger-point and a come-hither gesture from the clairvoyant. Finally, my turn to soldier up to the basement altar.

The old woman looked short from afar but up close, she made my tiny Italian granny seem like a redwood. And as if she wasn't short enough, the cigar-smoking clairvoyant was hunched over, looking like a human letter Q. Blowing cigar-smoke rings my way, she circled me as though she were scrutinizing a mid-century curio cabinet at a flea market. She spoke in Portuguese and her assistants translated.

She pointed to my knee and told me the injury I had was wished on me by someone I thought was a "friend," and she saw my mother and the one word she kept hearing was *inconvenient*. I had long pants on and didn't limp. How could she know I had an old skiing injury? And what did "inconvenient" mean? It freaked me out to say the least. This was a lot for the twenty-three-year-old me to grasp back then. After all, this wasn't Venice Beach or Haight-Ashbury, this was northern New Jersey. Yes, *that* North Jersey—not exactly the Mecca of transformational thinking.

The "quest" for me to someday park my horse in the I'm OK Corral would last from the 1970s through the '80s and '90s, up until my rock-bottom episode of 2017.

The Brain's Hemispheres

After all the decades I spent trying to fix myself, I eventually discovered why none of my efforts worked. Essentially, they were all external attempts to circumvent an internal issue. In other words, a left-brain logical solution to a right-brain emotional problem. Not only were my low self-esteem and overall sense I didn't belong formed in my right hemisphere, but because of how our brains function, they can only be tackled by the right. Not the left.

There are many theories about the left and right brain, about determining whether someone is a left- or right-brain thinker. It's more about which side you use more. For instance, if you're an engineer working on the problem of how water beads up on an airplane wing, you would be using left-side logic in the form of math and science. At the same time, you're using the creative right side to try different thoughts that don't usually belong together to find a solution. Could you put da Vinci in a box of right or left brain? You could, but you might end up looking foolish. Same goes for Einstein. Yes, we all use both sides of our brain. But that doesn't change which part of the brain is responsible for which activity. For that we revert to left-brain logic, right-brain emotion.

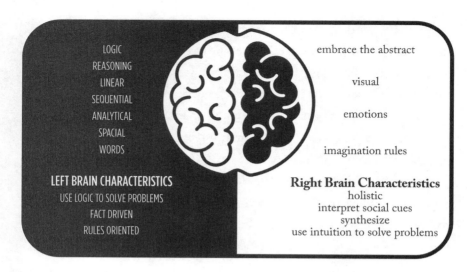

LOGIC
REASONING
LINEAR
SEQUENTIAL
ANALYTICAL
SPACIAL
WORDS

embrace the abstract

visual

emotions

imagination rules

LEFT BRAIN CHARACTERISTICS
USE LOGIC TO SOLVE PROBLEMS
FACT DRIVEN
RULES ORIENTED

Right Brain Characteristics
holistic
interpret social cues
synthesize
use intuition to solve problems

The left side of the brain is associated more with logic and rationality, and the right controls creativity and emotion. As you can see by the chart above, facts, rules, logic, and reasoning form on the left side, and imagination, emotions, intuition, and the abstract are formed on the right. A good example of how this works is someone who has been diagnosed with ASD (formerly known as Asperger's syndrome) having difficulty making eye contact and interpreting gestures during conversations. Interpreting social cues is a function of the right hemisphere. I spent several years volunteering with adults with autism and Asperger's and understand that it is a result of underdevelopment in the right hemisphere, making the left hemisphere dominant, which is why people with Asperger's are great with numbers, facts, logic, and analytics but are unaware of even the most basic social cues and often have poor body coordination, which is also a right-brain function. Autism is the opposite end of the spectrum. It is a result of the underdevelopment of the left hemisphere.

For decades I was searching for answers from dozens of well-meaning self-help books, gurus, therapy, life coaches and seminar after seminar. But they were all approaching my "issues" from a logical, left-brain point of view.

A perfect example of this are things that I heard dozens, maybe hundreds of times in my decades of self-fixing. Stop negative thinking, forgive yourself, stay positive, love yourself, see yourself as worthy, try to relax, concentrate on your good qualities, don't beat yourself up, stop being a people-pleaser . . . I've heard them all and more. The negative thought patterns were just a symptom of the bigger issue. But what was the issue? I was not only clueless, but the so-called answers kept coming. Let's just say telling someone like me to just change how I was thinking and suddenly love myself or stay positive and that will cure my ills was ludicrous. Not one of my self-fix attempts said anything about why I have these low self-esteem issues. Unless you count the therapist who focused on my mom teaching me to do my own laundry at nine or the seminar that pointed to that aha moment when my mom yelled at me as my why. They weren't. Those self-fix solutions all were linear, left-brain rules to follow. They never worked, nor will they ever.

That only kept me searching for more. And always coming up empty. Little did I realize that my "issues" were not logic- or left-brain based but rather stemmed from emotions that began at a very early age. A right-brain emotional, holistic issue. I was attempting to solve a right-brain issue with a left-brain solution. The result was decades of disappointment and frustration.

Was all the "searching" worth it? Hard to say. But I *can* say the ten thousand hours I spent trying to find myself by reading those hundreds of thousands of words still left me in search of more.

I have shared these vignettes from my seemingly never-ending days of pain, perpetual confusion and inner conflict to give you a small glimpse into where I came from and to hopefully put the following account of my voyage in perspective. In writing this section, I had to return to parts of my past that I wasn't too fond of. But I believe everything does happen for a reason. For instance, reliving my experiences with life coaches brought back a question that all three often raised: *Where do you want to be down the road?* I had absolutely no idea then. My answer now is quite simple. "I don't know, but it doesn't matter. What I do know without a doubt is that I will be completely OK with myself when I get there."

3

The Perpetual Gutter Ball

I have a twin sister. Not huge news, but the novelty surprisingly fascinates folks. Our parents included. Like it or not, we often would receive twin presents. When we were eleven, we both got bowling balls for Christmas.

Our mom bowled and was a coach/administrator for the junior league my sister and I were in. Our league was about to gear up, and mom booked a lane for a practice game. Coach Mom rolled first, and was impressive as usual. My sister grabbed her new ball and studied the alley. Her footwork and form were in keeping with what Coach Mom had drilled into her. Her execution seemed flawless. That was until halfway down the alley, when the ball tailed hard left and banged loudly into the gutter. Ball number two— same form, same slide, same release, same—BAM! Gutter ball. A side glance and pursed lips from Mom, and we moved on.

Once my sister's turn came around again, Coach Mom couldn't hold back: "Keep your thumb straight and follow through," she instructed. My sister did, to no avail. As if it were three gutter balls and you're out, Coach Mom jumped up, emphatically declaring, "You have to follow through! It's simple! If the thumb is straight, the ball will go straight."

In obvious frustration, Coach Mom grabbed my sister's ball and stepped up to demonstrate. With complete conviction and determination, Coach Mom let the ball go in textbook form. The ball got halfway down the alley until crashing into the left gutter even more loudly than my sister's had. We wanted to laugh but didn't want to incur the wrath of "the coach."

It turned out that the new ball my sister got for Christmas was defective. No, it wasn't square or rectangular or anything, but it was out of balance, somehow ever so slightly heavier on one side. No way it could ever be counted on to perform the way it was designed to. No way anyone could get a winning score with that ball. The game was rigged. On the outside, the new ball appeared perfectly round. Three flawlessly spaced, smooth and comfortable holes. It felt normal, and from the perspective of everyone around it, there was nothing to be concerned about.

The 7 Word Story we have all created for ourselves is very much like that bowling ball. It sounds right. Looks right. Feels right. And is well-designed. It should work like a charm. But like the out-of-balance blue-and-black marble globe, it's a setup. We were all completely unaware of the inner-balance issues the ball had just as we are oblivious and unaware of how our unconscious minds sabotage us daily. Our inner 7 Word Game consistently drops us into the gutter without any visible reason why. Yet we keep rolling that ball down, over and over, hoping it will yield different results.

Our current culture has convinced us that most of what we think, say and do is done consciously, that what we say is what we mean, and that what we see is authentic, true, and real. The unconscious 7 Word Story running our lives wants us—needs us—to believe it is also true, reliable, and authentic. Like my sister's unbalanced Christmas present, it's a guaranteed gutter ball.

From BC to AD (Before Consciousness to Awareness Discovered)

"Until you make the unconscious conscious, it will direct your life and you will call it fate." This prophetic observation inspired by Carl

Jung, protégé and favored disciple of Sigmund Freud, is in many ways the inspiration and foundation for the 7 Words and the rest of the words in this book.

Jung founded analytical psychology, or Jungian analysis, and made astonishing breakthroughs regarding the empirical science of the psyche. He believed that in its basic form, wholeness is becoming aware of our unconscious thinking and how it plays out in our lives. Wholeness and oneness are achieved only when there is harmony between the conscious and unconscious. We have all heard the words conscious, unconscious, consciousness, and unconsciousness before. So where does consciousness come from?

Scientists, theologians, and philosophers have been baffled by that very question for centuries. It remains one of the biggest unknowns across all of science. There's even some debate within the scientific community whether consciousness continues after death. While I'm not promising you the answers of the universe here, or even pretending that I have found what the secret philosophers and scientists have been scratching their heads over for centuries, what I will be exploring throughout this book is how our unconscious mind has played a major role in many of our actions throughout our life and how those actions have sabotaged us, especially when it comes to our relationships with others and ourselves.

Decades of my life were spent counterfeiting—metaphorical tender, that is. In retrospect, spending all those years fabricating a version of myself seems like a crime. Attempting to convince others, mostly myself, that I had my crap together. That nothing "bothered" me and I was this happy, easygoing guy. There was a reason for all that. My little dark secret was that I had a story. An unconscious script I had to stick to. I had absolutely *no* clue about my own forging, faking, or fabricating. But there was a perpetual soft, underlying *hum* of discontent or dissatisfaction running through me for as far back as my memory can take me that echoed the feeling of being irrelevant or undeserving. Decades were spent attempting to figure out why I couldn't get my crap together like seemingly everyone else who crossed my path or whom I viewed from afar. In retrospect, the examining and searching was a conscious act, but all my conscious searching for all those years and decades led to only one thing: more searching. But the answers were unconscious—inside me, and not outside where I was looking.

While we are fully aware of what is going on in the conscious mind, we have no idea of what information is floating around in our unconscious self. Our conscious mind works as if solving a math problem. We see $10 + 15 + 5 + 9 + 3 - 32 = 10$. We can somehow pull that learned ability up because we have a reference point inside our brain. If we never learned how to add or subtract, we would not be able to figure out the answer to that problem. We would have no foundation to draw from. This would fall under the category of stored knowledge as shown in the illustration below. Memories, in contrast to active, applied knowledge, are easily accessible if we just dive deep below the water level. Everything in our mind is available to us; we just have to bring it up to the surface.

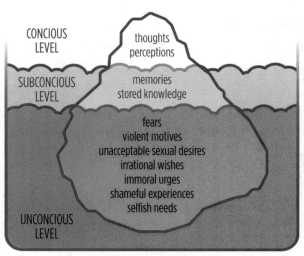

CONCIOUS LEVEL

thoughts
perceptions

SUBCONCIOUS LEVEL

memories
stored knowledge

fears
violent motives
unacceptable sexual desires
irrational wishes
immoral urges
shameful experiences
selfish needs

UNCONCIOUS LEVEL

FREUD'S MENTAL ICEBERG (1915)

Sigmund Freud also viewed the unconscious as a reservoir of memories and information, something we can't ignore. "The unconscious mind," he clarified, "is the primary source of human behavior." As illustrated in Freud's famous mental iceberg model most of what we as humans feel and act upon is inaccessible to our conscious self. Ten percent of our behaviors or actions are known to us, while 90 percent of what drives those behaviors happens on an undetected level. It has been written of Freud's concept of the unconscious self, "Thoughts and emotions outside of our awareness continue to exert an influence on our behaviors, even though we are unaware (unconscious) of these underlying influences."[1] Like our 7 Word Story, most of what occurs is happening in our underwater unconscious.

With 90 percent of our behavior occurring below the surface, it becomes nearly impossible to be in touch with it. Not to mention many of our so-called unconscious thoughts and actions were formed or created when we were young and impressionable. As we grow up, some of this learning becomes conscious understanding while much of it reverts to the climate-controlled storage unit of our unconscious. Have you ever noticed how kids are creative, energetic, imaginative machines, and most adults, well, aren't? That's because most of that learning, imagining, creating, and experiencing is shifted from the conscious to our unconscious mind. If you recall, only 10 percent of our mind is conscious, and everything else rests below the surface. Most of the underwater unconscious is running on autopilot, and we are "unaware," which is precisely what *unconscious* means.

We end up repeating a pattern found in our early childhood that got us the result that every child wants: to feel loved and get attention. When we become adults, we never give up mirroring this story we created in our unconscious as children, which remains unavailable to our conscious self.

But once we know about this story that we made up as a three-year-old (and why the age of three, we will discuss in the next chapter) and how it has sabotaged our relationships and self-esteem, it will be impossible to unknow it.

We will finally be able to drive the bus ourselves and let our unconscious 7 Words sit in the back. Moving and acting with intention and purpose, handling everything that comes at us from a place of strength and understanding. We suddenly become present. We just handle every moment as it shows up and, with direct intention, decide what comes next. We're true to ourselves, which is something we could never experience being unconscious, and that's the greatest gift we can give ourselves.

How do we get there? Well, we have to make the unconscious conscious, and the best way to do that is through mindfulness.

Unconscious and Conscious, Meet Sentience

According to Western philosophy, "sentience" is defined as the capacity to experience feelings and sensations. When we are unconscious, we don't feel. We just do. We automatically react, mostly responding the same way we have always responded. Being conscious, on the other hand, is knowing or being aware of and responding to one's surroundings as they are.

Let's face the facts: most of us never learned how to identify our feelings, never mind how to deal with them. We learned to bury all those suckers because they seem so scary. But burying doesn't work. Some attempt to drown their feelings in alcohol, but those crazy little feeling critters figure out how to swim. Others attempt to bury feelings with shopping, overworking, sex, working out, staying constantly busier than everyone they know and—here's a popular one—by putting all their energy into taking care of and doing, doing, doing for everyone else. Those who want to be an anchor for everyone else usually find themselves the one who ends up drowning. Burying our feelings can also be like trying to get rid of a weed in a garden: you can dump truckload after truckload of dirt over it, but it will find its way back to the surface. Just like how our pesky feelings eventually do.

So, why didn't our parents teach us how to handle our emotions and feelings? For the same reason their parents couldn't teach them. One can only pass on what one knows. As children, most of us learned early on that we couldn't distinguish what we were feeling. It was completely foreign to us. Even if we stumbled onto something, my family growing up was all about "Don't ask, don't tell" when it came to emotions and feelings. And even on the off chance we came close, our parents couldn't help much because *frightful feelings* were not something they were good at facing for themselves, much less for their children. No wonder they were unable to comfort us. Imagine we're three years old, and we go to Mom or Dad and drop this gem in their lap: "Mom, Dad, I feel like I need more love and attention from you. The world is beginning to feel scary, and I just want you to hold me and be there for me emotionally. Hug me, tell me everything is going to be OK. Squeeze me, love me, and accept me unconditionally." Yes, that's a great fantasy. Maybe in our next life.

We all have this unconscious story we carry around with us that is impossible to change unless we first become aware of it. In other words, make it conscious. Which is why when that Jung quote about making the unconscious conscious pierced my brain, it was as though I finally got Carl Jung. More like his words got me! At that moment I understood. There's a difference between knowledge and understanding. Knowledge is information that can be passed on or shared. Understanding is visceral; it's an intuitive, instantaneous experience you feel in your gut.

But there is something we can start now, and that is becoming conscious of those "frightful feelings," bringing them to our awareness.

And the best way to do that is simple: stop thinking. Stop searching. Instead, start feeling. *Feeling* allowed me to become aware of the external and internal worlds that were previously whizzing past me. In turn, that awareness led to mindfulness. If you're wondering if you can have awareness without mindfulness, the answer is yes. But not the other way around. Awareness is the precursor to mindfulness. Awareness is being in the moment and noticing everything going on inside and outside of us. Mindfulness is noticing everything going on inside and outside of us and letting it all pass by or through us without judging any of it.

When I finally allowed myself to feel, which led to awareness then mindfulness, I finally discovered that happiness, sadness, joy, sorrow and pain were just borrowed feelings. None were meant to be owned or coveted. Once I began treating them like the passing clouds they truly are, mindfulness ensued! And I have meditation to thank for that.

The Benefits of Meditation

"One does not become enlightened by imagining figures
of light, but by making the darkness conscious."
—Carl Jung[2]

As I was writing this book, I Googled "Meditation is good for you." I found an article that offered twenty reasons why meditation is good for us. Stopping just short of sounding like an article from *The Onion*, here are some of the "reasons" the article gave to meditate: It could help people with arthritis. Makes music sound better. Helps your doctor be better at their job. Makes you a better person. Helps troops perform better. Supports your weight loss. Comes in handy during cold season. Makes your grades better.

Wow! Nothing can live up to that list. Meditation isn't intended for those purposes to begin with. These sorts of expectations only help leave anyone considering meditation feeling intimidated, insecure, and like a loser when they don't experience the results everyone is yapping about.

When we convince ourselves that what we think, focus on, or believe we want will be the fruits of our meditative labors, we are all about attachment to an outcome and nothing else, bringing us back to the unhappiness we set out to "cure" through meditating in the first place.

Meditation is a conscious act we choose to connect to our unconscious self. It sounds a bit oxymoronic, or possibly just moronic, but it's not. It's a retreat to the quite corner of our own being. A sanctuary where we're able to overcome our reoccurring nemesis: thinking! For decades I buried and deflected my feelings using humor as an avoidance tactic in the hope the feelings would magically dissolve. They didn't. Instead, they festered and burrowed deeper into the vault. The ultimate facing of my feelings crumbled the facade and took the tomb walls with it. It finally got me to stop trying to lean into everything and instead, rest in awareness.

> *"You don't understand, my brain*
> *won't slow down. It's not for me."*
> **—Every single person before they learned to meditate**

Often, and I've seen this with a lot of people who are just starting out with meditation, we get disenchanted after just a few minutes of trying. From experience, I know all too well how insanely long even one minute of *trying* to silence our brain can be.

For more than twenty years, I "attempted" meditation, and each time came up with the same conclusion: *I suck at this! Nothing can slow down this mighty overthinking contraption between my ears.*

Apparently, every person who has ever meditated—or tried to—has said the exact same thing. When someone would attempt to reassure me that my mind was no different than anyone else's and, in fact, was quite capable of slowing enough to meditate, my smartass self would repeat the words of the philosopher Bugs Bunny, "What a maroon!"

Where did all that negativity come from? What kept whispering, "Jerry, you can't possibly meditate . . . your brain is just too *busy* or *active* to do that crap"? It was surprising to find that the long-awaited answer to where this sabotage was coming from was my ego.

Yup! My ego not only embraced the chatter in my brain, but it also fueled it. There was no better saboteur. The ego—yours and mine—tries to convince us that a quiet mind is a useless mind. And my mind bought into this insanity for decades. Everywhere we look, people are telling us we need to do more. Society, the media, and social media all tell us what we should be thinking, wearing, driving, eating, dining, reading, where to travel, and where to buy a house or city to move to. Much of all this is based on our need for approval, to be noticed and feel like we're somehow enough. Ego is the limousine driver of those needs.

Our ego constantly tries to convince
us its only mission is to keep us safe.

Translation: *Scared!*

After decades of lame attempts, I un-made-up my mind and sat there. Just sat.

This was the beginning of October 2016, shortly before the crash that set me off to find My 7 Words. I had watched an interview with a master teacher who taught thousands how to meditate. She confessed that after forty years of practice, her mind still wanders. *Wow, if a veteran of immeasurable hours of meditation still had her mind occasionally wander, what would stop me now?* It was time to go for it and see what happened.

Meditation is the Enemy of Ego and the Way to Our Unconscious Self

We meditate so our souls can catch up. During that quiet time, there is no structure. No objective. No predetermined outcome. For me, it's just sitting, back straight, head straight, with my spine and shoulders relaxed and my eyes gently shut, looking straight ahead as though peering through my closed eyelids. I usually set my phone timer for seventeen minutes. Why seventeen? Can't really say. I sat down early in my practice and thought ten or fifteen minutes seemed not right, and twenty was too round. Something said seventeen was it. Sometimes for a quick midday meditation, nine or twelve minutes will do the job. At some point, I began using eye shades and noise-canceling headphones to block out the world. My ego tried to sabotage the process by calling that cheating; I call it using any tools to help me quiet my mind.

This is my practice. You may decide on a different amount of time. Or sit on the floor, a straight-back chair, or whatever you feel comfortable with. Though guided meditation or music is very distracting for me, it certainly works for others. This is worth repeating: you can't do it wrong! Hearing that was a game changer. Just the act of sitting still for even five minutes is an accomplishment. There are times when clicking into a peaceful zone happens within seconds. Minutes. Or only moments before the alarm goes off. Or not at all. So what? It doesn't matter. There are no bad or good meditations. There are only ones we do and ones we don't do. Simple. That's why it's a meditative *practice*, not a competition.

For those of you who are in desperate need of a rule, there is just one. Our back or spine—the main axis of our body—needs to be straight. However you decide to make that happen is fine. A straight back or spine not only keeps your heart and lungs open, making it easier to breathe, but it opens a path through which the chakra energy can more easily flow in both an upward and downward direction. There are seven major chakras or energy centers (yes, another lucky 7) with five of them located along the spine, starting with the lowest root chakra located at the base of our spine and ending at the throat chakra. The other two are the third-eye chakra at the middle of the forehead and the crown chakra at the top of the head.

Early on, my ego tried to get me to meditate lying down, but it didn't work. "Beditation," as I call it, has a more common label: sleep! Some claim that sleep is meditation. Or gardening. That's also our ego's way of manipulating us into not meditating. Ego hates meditation. Ego can't control us during meditation. Nothing to attach to or thoughts to hijack, corrupt, or manipulate.

Is meditation mindfulness? One way to put it is that meditation is a practice we do to allow us to eventually become mindful. They are interconnected in many ways. Meditation is a garden tool that tills the soil so mindfulness can flourish. It frees us from the daily overthinking and ego-driven preconceptions. Mindfulness is a result of the letting go, which meditation has gifted us, so we achieve clarity in our decision-making and our daily lives.

Mindfulness is about allowing ourselves to absorb and engage our feelings, emotions, and present-moment experiences as they occur. The key is to do so without rating or judging them and understanding that things are neither good nor bad: they just are. Often in early meditative sessions, we may experience upsetting feelings or emotions that we've suppressed for so many years. I certainly had my share during many a session. They appear to jump out at us and seem overwhelming at first, but we soon learn they're not menacing at all. Just unfamiliar.

Our ego hates for us to face those feelings or any real feelings. And for good reason—it can't control the narrative. The old saying "We have nothing to fear but fear itself" comes to mind. When we allow our feelings to emerge from the dark cave, the powerful light of self-awareness magically dissolves away any fear. We then discover that the feelings and emotions we have been petrified of for so long have no real power. It took me some time to get there. For me, having been run by my ego my whole life hadn't gotten me any peace whatsoever. Plus, I was already at rock bottom, so I finally just let go and trusted the process. There was nothing else to lose or no place lower to be.

Most people don't meditate. Maybe you've tried and given up or never attempted it. While I highly recommend diving into this, you *do not* have to meditate, know how to, or even entertain the thought of it to get to your 7 Word Story. Yes, it is the process by which I uncovered my own story. *My* process. Is it my belief your life would be somehow improved by a meditative practice? Absolutely! Is it my intention to scare you off by talking about it? Hell no! So, take all the meditation references that follow as an example of *my* process. If it helps nudge you to try it, that's great. If not, that's great, too. Just know that if some sarcastic, cynical, overthinking, recovering Catholic and self-proclaimed smartass from the anti-transformation, anti-mindfulness capital of the world—northern New Jersey—can do it, someone with way less carry-on baggage like you can as well. Trust me.

The way I see it: Prayer is talking
to your higher spirit or higher self.
Meditation is your higher self/spirit talking to you.

Three separate but critical meditations took place in the early months of 2017, while I was uncomfortably ensconced at the bottom of my dark hole. Though seemingly unrelated, the following became the keystone of my unconscious story.

Meditation One

Sitting in my usual morning meditation spot, soon after my mind cleared, a scene appeared from the movie *City Slickers*. It's about three friends going through their midlife crises together and deciding to leave New York City for two weeks to become cowboys and drive a herd of cattle from New Mexico to Colorado.

In the scene, the city slicker Mitch, played by Billy Crystal, was riding his horse next to the crusty old cowboy named Curly, played by Jack Palance. Both are slowly plodding along on their horses when Curly turns and says:

CURLY: Do you know what the secret of life is?

MITCH: No. What?

CURLY: This. (*Curly holds up his index finger.*)

MITCH: Your finger?

CURLY: One thing. Just one thing. You stick to that and everything else don't mean s—t!

MITCH: That's great, but . . . what's the one thing?

CURLY: That's what you gotta figure out.

And just like that, the scene was over. Nothing else from that meditation stuck with me. Nothing else mattered. One thing? What one thing? I had no idea, but I logged in my journal anyway.

Meditation Two

A week or so later, same routine, same spot, same seventeen minutes on the timer. This time I heard a voice. Not a recognizable voice. Not a famous actor or familiar voice-over. Just a voice, loud and clear, saying, "You gave away your power your whole life, so other people would like you and love you!" That was it for that meditation.

Freaked out? No. Confused? Maybe. Excited? Absolutely! And thinking to myself, "This could me my one thing. It sounds like a one-thing sorta thing. But what does it mean? Just write it down!" And I did.

Most times my meditations are filled with silence. Nothing but calm. Sometimes there are colors. Chakra colors that move in and out like waves. The colors caught me off guard at first, but I've come to appreciate their presence. Colors, quiet, calm, visions or peace, no matter what, the idea is to simply take what shows up. Or not. No expectations. Just trust the process. Trust the universe.

In this case, the universe was leaving me a specific message: I gave my power away my whole life so people would like or love me! An important, relevant dot on my journey of discovery, which we'll soon be connecting. But for now, it was just a random statement.

Meditation Three

The next dot came a good week or two later. This time another vision. Not a movie, more of a livestream eavesdropping. The setting was Town Lake in downtown Austin, Texas. The visualization was of an adult male walking with a little kid, and they were holding hands. I was walking fifteen or twenty feet behind them.

They approached a park bench, turned, and sat. To my surprise, the adult on the bench was the current me in 2017. An even bigger shock: the little boy was me too! My own mini-me who was roughly three or so years old. Blonde crew cut, goofy crooked smile and all. Little jerry sat on the park bench overcome with tears. The man next to him, Big Jerry, asked, "Why are you crying?" Little jerry pleaded, "I can't do it anymore. I'm so tired. I've been doing it for so long; I just can't carry it anymore. Please help me." Big Jerry whispered, "It's OK. It's going to be all right. You don't have to do it anymore. I will help take this pain away from you. I promise."

Dot. Dot. Dot.

I sat with my trio of meditations for a week or two, waiting to see if another puzzle piece might show. Nothing appeared. I was back to the safety of my quiet meditation space. Nothing but the sounds of silence. Even the broken waterpipes of uncontrollable tears were dissipating. In fact, at some point not too soon after this flurry of information, the tears stopped altogether, just as unexpectedly as they had begun. The reservoir—or better yet, the swamp—was now dry. I had cried for all the reasons I needed to and was now cleansed. Lighter. I didn't know it then but I'm certain today I will never cry for those same reasons again. I was at peace with those tears. But there was more to do.

I became obsessed with connecting those meditations, those three dots. But first, I needed to inspect them. I was positive these weren't dreams or predictions, but just as convinced they were significant. Our meditations don't mean anything to anyone but us. They are connected to a pathway to our own individual Higher Consciousness and furthermore, our connection to the universal "Higher" power. My job was to decipher the treasure map. But where was I to start? When we were kids, we had a page with a bunch of numbered dots, and we just took our No. 2 pencil and went in order. By dot number fifty-six, you had a perfect outline of an elephant. Or a Christmas tree. If only.

I went back to my days in advertising as a copywriter and Creative Director. Just like back then, I was starting with a blank page. Inspiration was needed.

As I had always done in the past, I trusted my gut and my experience with some help from my muse—meditation. That's when it hit me. The ending of the last meditation was by far the most emotional and intense of all with little jerry in tears. It seemed like he was almost calling out to me. *Start at the end and work backwards.* I needed some reverse engineering to find what little jerry was so upset over. What was he carrying? What was he so tired about that he couldn't do it anymore? How young was he? I meditated on it and thought back to the nine years I spent at the West LA preschool my three kiddos had attended and deduced that little jerry was roughly three years old. And that is exactly where my search began. I was about to discover what three-year-old little jerry had been carrying around for all those many decades. I was determined to give him clarity, understanding, and acceptance. And some well-deserved peace. What I didn't know then was that Big Jerry was about to be receiving those same gifts.

4

The Magic Age

Would you let a three-year-old govern your romantic relationships? Make personal decisions that impact you? Your family? Would you allow a three-year-old to run your life? Well, most of us do just that every day. Not knowingly or intentionally, of course, but that's exactly what happens.

The entire premise for Your 7 Words begins at the research level, which shows that the magic age for children, all of us, is roughly three. Beginning at three, our development takes a giant leap. It's a period of rapid growth, especially in our cognitive abilities. Our personalities develop and emerge. We ask interesting, thoughtful questions as our attention span increases. Our sorting, organizing, and matching abilities are honed. Symbols or language skills are present, memory and imagination are developed. Nonreversible and nonlogical thinking emerge. Children show intuitive problem-solving skills and begin to grasp relationships and the concept of numbers. And let's not forget: it's the age where egocentric thinking predominates.

Charles Darwin (1809–1882) spent a great deal of time and energy on the study of child development. In fact, his work "A Biographical Sketch of an Infant" is thought of as one of the first infant psychology studies. Darwin did most of his research and writing from his quiet, rural home in Kent, where he and his wife Emma enjoyed ten children together. For many years, he studied his children and kept extensive journals on their growth and progress. According to the Darwin Correspondence Project at Cambridge University, "The notes he made while watching his own children grow up were the principal source of information for much of his understanding of human development."

> *"Once I asked Mr. Darwin which of the years*
> *of a child's life were the most subject to incubative*
> *impressions,' said Richmond [Darwin's portrait artist].*
> *His answer was, 'Without doubt, the first three.'"* [1]

We're not certain why Charles Darwin believed that children at age three were the most subject to impressions. His focus seemed to be more toward the bigger picture. The very big one. But whatever he saw, it's not much different today than it was when he first began his observations of children in 1839. Preschoolers (age 3–4) still find themselves in a transitional place leaving toddlerdom behind and attempting to navigate a confusing path to kindergarten. In retrospect, we (my twin sister and I) and really, all of us, as different and similar as we are, experienced this magical, mystical and transformative time in our young lives. As I collected and inspected the dots of what I'm calling age three—but may technically be somewhere between ages 3–4—I discovered things that fascinated, sometimes frightened, but forever changed me. Let's just say I'll never look at a three-year-old the same way again. Especially considering I now know this is when our 7 Words are formed.

Three-Year-Olds' Brains

At age three, we have nearly twice as many synapses as in adulthood. Synapses are the "connectors" that transfer messages between neurons in the brain. More precisely, they are the microscopic gaps in between neurons that transport the messages along the channel. These "gaps" allow nerve impulses to pass from one neuron to another, carrying the messages back and forth between different parts of the brain in a process called "neurotransmission."

During the first three years of life, a child's brain undergoes an unprecedented amount of change, especially regarding synapses. They're formed faster during these first three years than any other time. In fact, there is so much growth that there are twice as many at age three than we will have or need as an adult.[2] They communicate to each other via a superhighway of up to a quadrillion (which is a 1 with fifteen zeroes) connections. This is twice the number of connections in the adult brain you're using to read this. Imagine three-year-old us going to our parents and telling them, "Give me a break, I'm overloaded. I have a quadrillion connections going on in my brain right now." Can't you hear our parents' response to that gem? *I told you a million times, don't exaggerate!*

Our brain at that age is also nearly twice as active as it will be in adulthood. The child's brain is a dense jumble of wiring and creates a sort of super magnet to external input. Experiences are drawn in and absorbed at a much higher rate than any other time in our development. This surplus eventually becomes overwhelming, excessive, and ultimately needs to be trimmed away. Ever see a three-year-old at a park? They don't stop. Constant motion. Their bodies are just following the lead of the perpetual-motion machine working overtime inside their heads.

According to the Urban Child Institute, neuroscientists have found that synaptic density in the prefrontal cortex probably reaches its peak during our third year, up to 200 percent of its adult level.

Our surplus connections are gradually purged throughout childhood and adolescence. The medical term for the trimming process is "synaptic blooming and pruning." Throughout this process, our brain is molding or shaping itself. Not relying on genetics alone, we're absorbing through experiences and input from many exterior sources. The scientific community refers to this as "plasticity."

> *"The excess of synapses produced by a child's brain in the first three years makes the brain especially responsive to external input. During this period, the brain can 'capture' experience more efficiently than it will be able to later, when the pruning of synapses is underway."* [2]
> **—Peter R. Huttenlocher, MD**

Let's say the more we practice the piano, speak a language, or even juggle, the stronger those circuits get. Our brains are like a synaptic garden growing connections between neurons. The more we water and cultivate them, the stronger they become. And, sticking to that analogy, when we don't use them or "cultivate" them, our brain will eliminate—or in another gardening analogy, "prune off"—those connecting pathways, making space in our brain garden for new growth. So, turns out, our *three*nager self is processing too much information, not too little.

Compared to the three-year-old who has around one thousand trillion synapses, a teenager will have around five hundred trillion, which remains relatively the same into adulthood.[3] When we compare threenagers who are experiencing nearly double the number of synapses they will have during adulthood with *teen*agers who are at the height of synaptic pruning, some things become clear. Parents of both threenagers and teenagers are being driven crazy by threens who won't sleep and teens who can't get enough sleep. Obviously, the first three years of life are an exciting, stimulating, and growth-filled time in our development. We all go from helpless, entirely dependent newborn blobs to overactive and magical overcommunicating toddlers, then ultimately to rebellious teens who can talk but choose not to.

Imagination

Our imagination also becomes fully born around age three, when we create imaginary worlds with imaginary friends to inhabit them. My imaginary friends were Maynor and Jaynor. Being a twin, it's not surprising my imagination would conjure a pair of made-up pals. At that age, we also impart stuffed animals, dolls, and toys with names, traits, and personalities.

Magical Thinking

Magical thinking, the belief that our words or even thoughts can influence the world around us, also begins around age three. A toddler engaged in magical thinking believes he or she can create outer experiences from their inner imagination or feelings. As an example, when Manny puts on a Superman costume, others see Manny in a costume. In Manny's mind, he *is* Superman. Same goes for Mary Beth. It's Mary Beth's kingdom, and you will listen to her because she *is* the princess.

It's an extremely magical age when cognitive abilities begin to take shape. It's also the time children begin believing in Santa Claus, the Tooth Fairy, and the like. Before age three, we simply don't have the capability to create that story. At three, it's our world, and we allow others to live in it.

At this age, a child will essentially believe by simply *thinking* something, it will magically mold their world around them into whatever they want. This is along the same lines as imagination. At three, we are full of doubt, possibly for the first time. Our confused new "reality" sees to it that if we have any doubt that we are loved, we will "fix" it with magic-think! As you will see later, magic-think is a cornerstone of the 7 Word Story process.

> *"Magic thinking is a normal part of child development . . . A child may believe her 'jealous feelings' caused her brother to fall off the swing . . . [and that] she will fly like a fairy and find her missing kitten outside; that the rainbow happened because of her powerful wishes . . . The [child] brain is not yet equipped to differentiate inner from outer experience."*
> **—Barbara Dautrich, Professor of Education at American International College[4]**

Cause and Effect

Another big milestone is the cause-and-effect lightbulb turning on. It begins during the first year of life when babies start making primitive connections about what happened. I cried, and someone came to soothe me. At three, the toddler gets it.

> *"At around 36 months, children demonstrate an understanding of cause and effect by making predictions about what could happen and reflect upon what caused something to happen."[5]*
> **—California Dept. of Education**

At three, the child understands: If I put my hand on the stove, I will get burned. If I pull the dog's tail, the dog will bite me. If I push someone down on the playground, I will get punished. Important distinctions and connections are made.

John Stuart Mill, an influential British philosopher of the nineteenth century, wrote on logic, economics, and politics. In one of his most famous works, *The Greatest Happiness Principle*, Mill tells us, ". . . Utility, or the Greatest Happiness Principle, holds that actions are right in proportion as they tend to promote happiness, wrong as they tend to produce the reverse of happiness. By happiness is intended pleasure, and the absence of pain; by unhappiness, pain, and the privation of pleasure."[6]

In twenty-first-century terms, actions that produce pleasure or prevent pain are what we strive for and are most desirable. More pleasure + less pain = happiness. Run solely on instant or immediate gratification, the "pleasure principle" is driven by our unconscious need to fill our basic urges. How old are we when that all takes shape? Yup, you guessed it!

We had no ability to "think through" energy quests from age zero to age three. Crying got us attention/energy from others. Sometimes *not* crying and being good got us attention or energy from a mom or others. If I do Y (cause), then I'll get Z (effect) from Mom, Dad, whoever. At this age we also believe that if we leave cookies and milk for Santa Claus (cause), he will leave behind presents (effect). All this to say, early in life, we pick up signals from our environment about this exchange of energy and secretly absorb how it all works. Until age three, our brains aren't developed enough just yet to make those connections.

Influence and Ability to Lie

Stretching the truth, or lying, starts around age three. Why? Well, because at this point we can. We've discovered a newfound power over words as we come to the realization that adults can't read minds. It's a tricky learned ability because at three, most children haven't discovered how not to tip their hand. Nevertheless, they work at it. The game is to see how much they can get away with.

Emotions and Love

At three years old, our understanding of love is still developing. (Going out on a pretty firm limb, I don't know any adults whose understanding of love isn't also still a work in progress.) We may associate love with positive emotions such as feeling joy, safety, or comfort. We experience love through physical affection and may associate love with the people who provide us care and attention, such as parents or caregivers. This is what drives our third word—the lynchpin—of our 7 Word Story.

As we're developing, the lens we see our world through is based on the reflection of family, environment, and surroundings, but driven by our need for acceptance. As growing children, we never feel enough love. Especially unconditional love and acceptance. I'm not sure our parents or anyone could have given us enough love, which somehow makes it, almost by default, conditional. Some of that conditional love is used to "train" us—in other words, get us ready for the cruel real world by saying "Good job" when we don't wander off, talk to a stranger, or hesitate before running after a ball in the street. But as children, we internalize that loss or perceived loss of love not through a memory of words or actions, but through feelings. Those feelings persist through adulthood. The learned behavior that follows often leads to suppression of feelings to avoid consequences that don't bring about love and acceptance.

The Caregiver Split

At a certain point when we are young, it seems like overnight we have become split from our caregivers, especially our moms. Everywhere we turn, people are nudging us to be more independent—for us, as well as for them. We also want to be considered big. We want to do the big-kid stuff. The desire to be a big kid yet also have the protection and safety net of our caregivers creates a confusing dichotomy. Toddler development researchers Eve R. Colson, MD, and Paul H. Dworkin, MD, tell us, "Although toddlers strive for autonomy, issues of attachment remain important developmental themes."[7] Sure, we are gaining the faculties to be more independent (walk, run, communicate more complexly, think, ask questions), but we also miss the safety of our mothers/caregivers. Miss her, as in, *I want her attention.* Independence →Attention → Independence → Attention. Colson and Dworkin add, "Although he or she may wander, the toddler always is cognizant of the caregiver's presence and intermittently returns for reassurance."[8]

The threenager is undergoing unprecedented brain development. Along with the tremendous growth comes anger, frustration, emotional development, and plenty of confusion. If parents of three-year-olds find themselves confused about what their child is experiencing, get in line—the inmates are running the asylum. A three-year-old can't talk logic. Yes, their brains are 80 percent of an adult's, but many or most of the synaptic connections are bridges to nowhere. They understand cause and effect, but logic is well above their pay grade.

All the research on three-year-olds kept bringing me back to little jerry on the park bench saying, "I can't do this anymore. I'm so tired." What was he holding on to? What was he feeling he had to let go of? One thing became obvious: Big Jerry needed to continue connecting dots.

While I was doing all this dot connecting and piecing together, it all seemed to default not to the power of words but the unconscious, dominant influence of feelings. I began to understand my sleepwalker self not only as being unconscious of my actions but something worse—of my emotions. Logic can't change emotion . . . but emotions can alter logic. Bingo!

We all created this "connection" in our brain I'm calling our 7 Word Story, and it began at roughly three years of age. The cycle we formed with our words was used over and over and over again. Psychoanalysis and general therapy in the twentieth and twenty-first centuries often hunts, pecks, pokes and prods into the happenings of our past. Digging and scraping for incidents that can be pointed to as the aha moment when our lives went off the rails. The "thing" that screwed us up and continues to derail us into adulthood. The problem is, there usually isn't a single "event." Yes, some of us have experienced legitimately heinous, even evil happenings in our past. I've interviewed a number of people for this book who survived such traumatic horrors. Did those experiences influence their future adult selves? Absolutely. Did those events make them who they are today? No! All had their 7 Word Story in place by age three before most of these incidents even occurred. A narrative that becomes the continuous loop repeatedly playing in the unconscious mind. Looking back at the dots of my life, I didn't have a story—my story had me.

5

My 7 Words in Action

To find the key to my story, I turned to something called reverse engineering—taking something apart to examine its internal workings and mechanisms. By doing this, we get vital information about how an original design or product took shape. For instance, let's say a machine in a manufacturing plant breaks down. They've been running this workhorse for decades and have a huge investment at stake. Say one component of the assembly line fails, causing the entire line to shut down, and the company that originally supplied the equipment has since gone out of business. The options are to replace the entire assembly line with a costly new one or find a way to repair the single broken component. Taking a 3D image of the failed section allows for the identification of the issue and a blueprint for the creation of a replacement part. Reverse engineering can also be used in business settings to backtrack and uncover where a plan or strategy went off the rails. Or how the unintended consequences of a seemingly brilliant design ended in disastrous results.

In some ways, that's exactly how My 7 Words came to be. Not as scientifically or mechanically, but the thinking is the same. I was going through life repeatedly making decisions and responding to circumstances in certain ways. Maybe you know someone who seems to make the same mistakes or pick the same types of people over and over and suddenly—*surprise*—they're back in a bad relationship. Or the friend or family member who is never happy about anything, constantly waiting for their ship to come in, but it never does because they're waiting at the airport! The important question again is not *what* we did, but *why* we did it.

Let's take a trip down Sleepwalking Lane.

My 7 Words in Action

During the research and writing of this book, I did way more self-examination than I could have imagined possible. Many observations became dots for me to inspect as part of my connecting process. Originally, these pieces of my history were just events in my life before I became conscious. Just random. But now that I see them through the prism of my words, it completely changes how I perceive them. After you uncover your unconscious story, I recommend you look back at some incidents in your life with your specific words in mind. You'll see how your words played a role in your actions and the sometimes sabotaging of your relationships. Following are some stories that came back to me after I uncovered my words. I've omitted the stories highlighting the sabotaging of my romantic relationships—not because they were nonexistent, but because I wouldn't even know where to begin.

Story 1

I was roughly ten or eleven, and my friends and I were hanging out in Bobby's basement on Jefferson Street in Belleville, New Jersey, when one of us found Bobby's grandfather's haircutting tools. Immediately, the scissors, combs, aprons, and electric trimmers were laid out on the Ping-Pong table. We were ecstatic. Like kids in a barber shop. Then someone suggested we cut each other's hair. We all looked at each other, and when more glances came in my direction, I remember thinking, "Oh no, don't let them. Have someone else be the guinea pig." Soon they were begging and pleading. I wanted to say no, take a stand, but not wanting to rock the boat, I gave in and plopped on the wooden folding chair. From the moment my cheeks hit the rickety seat, I knew it was a mistake to give my power away to them, but I was petrified to say no.

Suddenly, I had three preteens hacking at my hair with different instruments. After one of them burned my neck with a hot comb, another fledgling stylist cut my ear with scissors. Now there was blood dripping on the apron. At that point, I was done. And no, I didn't leave a tip.

I can still see my mom's face when I got home. This happened to be the day before Easter. After she bandaged my bloody ear and her blood pressure finally came down, she cut the remaining hair on my head as best she could with "good" household scissors. My words had set me up and, like always, let me down.

Story 2

My twin sister was living in a dorm at the Fashion Institute of Technology in New York City. She asked if I could help her and her roommate move to an apartment near the Village, so I drove into "The City" from Jersey. When I got to the dorm, my sister and her roommate were walking out of their room in costume. Apparently, they were late for a Halloween party, so they wouldn't be "available" to help me move them. I loaded then unloaded their stuff in their new apartment by myself. If it had just been my twin sister, I might have left her stuff on Seventh Avenue. But I didn't want to make a scene with her roommate there. I was worried about what she would think of me, so I pushed all I was feeling as deep as it would go and moved them alone. Four hours later, I drove back to Jersey in Uncle Pat's borrowed dry cleaning delivery van, My 7 Words in tow.

Story 3

This last one was hard to relive. I had just started working for the NFL in New York as a creative director, and I had to supervise a video shoot at Giants Stadium during my home team's final game of the season. I was given an extremely rare NFL Films full access pass for the game, which meant I was free to go anywhere in the stadium before, during, and after the game. This included my childhood team's locker room. But I had promised a good friend I would go with her to her work Christmas party that evening and didn't want to disappoint her by being late picking her up even though the party was going to last for many hours.

I remember feeling incredibly torn between a once-in-a-lifetime chance to visit the Giants locker room with all my favorite players and rushing out to take my friend to her party. Now I know what those strange feelings going through me were: my words.

I never stepped foot in the locker room after the game, and I regret it to this day. A once-in-a-lifetime opportunity gone. The game's final score was Giants–35, Chiefs–21. My game's score: Words–7, Jerry–0.

The feelings I had during those times, and so many others, can't be brought back up. But I can still remember the discomfort as well as the frustration wondering why I kept on doing things I didn't really want to do. Why I continuously put other people's priorities and feelings ahead of mine. Why I was a perpetual people-pleaser. I had absolutely no idea why back then. Now it's crystal clear. Two of my words are LIKABLE and SUBORDINATE.

How a Bunch of Dots Became 7 Words

By now, I had been collecting and inspecting dots galore. I had dots about three-year-olds because little jerry was around that age. I had dots about why I gave up my power so people could like and love me. I had dots about life being just about that "one" thing. That's what I knew. Then one day, I re-stumbled upon a famous quote: "I've learned that people will forget what you said, people will forget what you did, but people will never forget how you made them feel." I instinctively knew that quote was not just a dot, but a connector to many—if not all—the others that came before it.

Sometimes the creative "fairy dust" is hidden in between the lines. This time, it was standing on tippy-toes waving like a madman. *People will never forget how you made them feel!*

With all these months of meditating, note-taking, and tears. Of researching, collecting, and banging my head on the metaphoric table, and now the solid dot from the wise quote above, it all came down to one question that became the answer: What was little jerry feeling when he said he couldn't do this anymore or carry this anymore? Now, can I explain how the "how you made them feel" concept became wedded to my quest? Not really. The closest explanation I could think of comes from a somewhat creative dude who made some pretty amazing connections in his day.

> *"Creativity is just connecting things. When you ask creative people how they did something, they feel a little guilty because they didn't really do it, they just saw something. It seemed obvious to them after a while. That's because they were able to connect experiences they've had and synthesize new things.'*
> **—Steve Jobs**[1]

The next serendipitous connection began courtesy of an online date. The hopeless romantic in me overruled everything I was dealing with and went on a date. It was a nice enough evening as these sorts of blind encounters go. I wasn't feeling it, not sure she was either, but we both made the effort. Over a plate of olives and cheese and a carafe of wine, she asked me, "Ever been to therapy?"

I replied that I had done four separate stints over the years.

She then asked if I'd done any inner-child work.

"I think that's illegal in New Jersey where I grew up . . . along with pumping your own gas." I smiled. She did not. Tough room.

Once the cheese was gone, we parted ways and wished each other a nice evening.

It was still early when I got home, so I turned to my *giant* obsession with little jerry. There were months of notes, journals, research, and observations strewn all over my desk and brain. I began asking, what does all this research have in common? In math terms, the lowest common denominator was toddlers. Preschoolers. Ages 3–4. Threenagers. I sat with it for a bit. Who or what was little jerry? A tiny me. A kid. A little child. A lost child with a large burden.

Then the question from my earlier date popped into my head. Had I ever done inner-child work? I had to admit I honestly didn't know what that meant. I did a swan dive into the rabbit hole. I searched "inner child." Finding my inner child, my wounded inner child, repairing it, reclaiming it.

My inner-child research led me to the person responsible for the term "inner child." The answer was Carl Jung. I knew of him, of course, but never read much of his work. That quickly changed. I immersed myself in Jung, his archetypes and his preoccupation with childlike inner feelings, as well as the mother archetype and the mother complex.

As I often do when attempting to learn more about something or someone, I look up their quotes. I find it's often a shortcut to the core of someone's beliefs or knowledge. I've been collecting quotes since the first Clinton administration with stacks of handwritten volumes to show for it. That night I scribbled one down on an index card:

> *"The mother-child relationship is certainly the deepest*
> *and most poignant one we know . . . the child is, so to*
> *speak, a part of the mother's body. Later it is part of*
> *the psychic atmosphere of the mother for several years,*
> *and in this way everything original in the child is*
> *indissolubly blended with the mother-image."* [2]
>
> **—Carl Jung**

Just as the word "feel" jumped from the aforementioned "people will never forget how you made them feel" quote, Jung's lightning bolt that night was "mother." Specifically, the mother-child relationship. It had been many hours since my date stuck that inner-child Post-it note inside my head. And as bleary as I was, my gut intuition was already drawing dot connections with permanent markers.

That next week, while studying my notes, it dawned on me there was a glaring disconnect between my research and my two recent dot discoveries—the "how you made them feel" quote, and Jung. My research regarding little jerry was very left-brain logic and fact-oriented. Cause and effect, brain size, neurons and synapses and ego. My new breakthroughs were all about feelings and relationships (mother-child), which are right-brain oriented. A small distinction, but an important one.

I had to take my logical, sequential, and rational left brain and my relationship-oriented, emotional, and intuitive right brain and come to a whole-brain solution that incorporated all the dots I was given before. It took me about two weeks to find my first word, but once that initial word came to me, the rest just seemed to roll off the assembly line.

At this moment, I was as unaware of where this was all going as you most likely are right now. You at least know there are seven words I was just attempting to use to somehow DIY myself out of my seemingly lifelong sleepwalk, if that was even possible. My intellectual and emotional dots were unfolding nicely and nothing at this point was going to get in the way.

My First Word

Here's how little jerry's story—my story—unfolded. Around age three, I was pinballing my way through life. Potty-trained, able to feed and dress myself like most. But my logical left brain had not yet developed, so I was running nonstop on emotions and desires. Now, I was a big boy, according to my mom and everybody around me. Mom needed me to be a big kid because by the time I was three, she was back in the infant sweepstakes with my new baby sister. Back to overnight feedings, nurturing, diaper changes. Let's just say, Mom was neck-deep in the 24/7 baby business. She needed me to be a big kid as much if not more than I wanted to be big and independent. But there was a hidden other part of me that didn't feel quite so independent. I wanted to climb the monkey bars by myself and play with the bigger kids, but I was scared. I needed to know that somehow Mom was still watching. I wasn't the self-sufficient creature I was portraying or everyone else wanted and needed me to be. I wanted and needed some reassurance (from Mom) that I was fine and going to be OK. More importantly, that I was safe. But Mom's attention reservoir was being drained by a new sibling, with little time or energy for me. "Safe" was not exactly what I was feeling. My irrational and emotional brain was craving independence, while at the same time still needing comfort and, more importantly, the attention from Mom I once received. Faced with that double-edged sword of need, I suddenly found myself confused and alone.

"People will never forget how you made them feel."

At about age three, everyone told me how independent I was, but I didn't feel it. When I wasn't getting the attention that not only I used to get but, almost as importantly, I *needed* to get to feel safe in this big-kid world, I had to ask myself a simple question: How did not getting the attention I wanted and needed from my mom make me feel? I thought about this for a while. Meditated on it. The sentiment was something akin to feeling alone. Feeling isolated. Maybe irrelevant. Well, I wasn't being seen. Not being seen sounds a lot like being invisible. That was the word that resonated with me at the time. I felt invisible.

This was not a logical response—remember at age three there is no logic going on. Just emotions and feelings. In my mind, my mom was too busy for me, wasn't paying attention to me, therefore I was *invisible*. It made complete sense.

My first word is *invisible*.

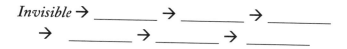

. . . But that same intuition knew this was not the entire story.

Second Word

The genie was now out of the bottle. Word #1 was in place and little jerry wasn't getting the attention he wanted and, more importantly, the attention he thought he needed from Mom, which made him feel *invisible*. Keep in mind, there's very little logic involved for little jerry or any of us at around age three. It's all about feeling.

Remember in chapter 3 where we talked about the research on three-year-olds? That is the age where cause and effect are beginning to make sense to us. If I put my hand on the stove, I will get burned. If I pull the dog's tail, it will bite me. In little jerry's mind, if X happens, then Y follows. Cause, then effect. I then extrapolated that theory out to this scenario. If little jerry felt *invisible*, what did *that* make him feel? I instinctively answered the question: If I felt alone, isolated . . . in other words, *invisible*, then what was the feeling that came next? If X was *invisible* then Y was_____?

Unloved.

My gut feeling was If I felt *invisible* that means I must be *unloved*. There it was . . . my second word was obvious. I felt *unloved*

My second word, and the second word of your story, is *unloved*.

Invisible → *Unloved* → _____ → _____ →
_____ → _____ → _____

Third Word

After uncovering these two words, it was impossible to concentrate on anything else. Nothing felt as important as solving this puzzle. I thought long and hard about those two words, which immediately got me thinking about my relationship with my mom. I knew my mom did indeed love me (albeit in her own way); I was just not getting the attention I desperately needed at that tumultuous time in my life.

I went back to the quotes I'd collected from Carl Jung. He had me covered: " . . . in every adult there lurks a child— an eternal child, something that is always becoming, is never completed, and calls for unceasing care, attention, and education. That is the part of the personality which wants to develop and become whole."[3]

For little jerry, invisible and unloved couldn't be the entire story. He wouldn't want to stay invisible or unloved; he would try to fix it.

And at age three, he tried fixing it with what he knew. Magic-think. "I'm magical," he reasoned. "I'll just change the way things are and get the attention and love I'm missing. Then I won't feel invisible and unloved anymore."

To get attention from my mom, I had to be or do something I thought or more likely felt would get her to pay attention to me. That was the end goal: get the needed attention. And love. We can't get love from someone unless we get their attention first. So, I asked myself how could I get my mom to pay attention to me? What do I feel would work?

The answer that surfaced was simple.

If I, Jerry, were only _____, my mom would pay attention to me. If she pays attention to me, she might like me. Then hopefully love me. This was the outcome I (we) ultimately want. And need. But first, I needed her attention somehow.

I sat at the kitchen table staring at a legal notepad with that *if I were only* statement scribbled on top in black Sharpie. The blank line was begging for an answer, but I was at a loss for words. Literally. This process began six hours ago over morning coffee and at this moment, I was sputtering. So I went into the bedroom and meditated. Twice. That got me to reboot and stop trying so damn hard. When I went back, my head was clear enough to try an old creative problem-solving trick: flip the question backwards, sideways, or upside down.

Instead of what I needed to be, maybe it was what I didn't, wouldn't, or couldn't do or want to be. I thought deeply about my mom, me growing up, with friends, in school, inside all my relationships, my marriages, my engagement with the penguin formally known as Jen. What did I not want, like, or want to be. It hit me: Confrontation. I hated it. Always have. Why? Well, I didn't feel safe. And something else—deep down I didn't want the other person to not like me. For any reason. I hated when anyone didn't like me. Holy s—t. *I have always hated it when people don't like me.* I grabbed the Sharpie and scribbled "*I* need to be liked. People need to like me." Too many words. Make it simpler.

Then I wrote the word. My word. *Likable.* I had to be *likable.* BAM!

If I, Jerry, were only *likable* , my mom would pay attention to me, then possibly love me.

That was what I always tried to be with Mom and everyone else in my life. Even strangers. At that exact moment, nothing felt more right to me. I felt the chasm between little and Big Jerry now had a bridge. I knew little jerry felt he had to be *likable* in order to get attention and love. And I knew that was his word because it was mine too. Has been since I was three. No wonder little jerry was so overwhelmed. And Big Jerry felt lost.

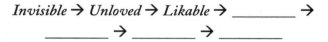

Invisible → Unloved → Likable → _____ →
_____ → _____ → _____

My third word became my mask, my persona that I began showing to the world while I was still little jerry: the roll-with-the-punches, go-with-the-flow, nothing-bothers-me Jerry was unknowingly my act so that people wouldn't disagree with me. They needed to like me. Which is why this quote from Marlon Brando is so eerily spot on: "Acting is the least mysterious of all crafts. Whenever we want something from somebody or when we want to hide something or pretend, we're acting. Most people do it all day long."[4]

This whole discovery process didn't have a blueprint to go by or reference points to compare it with. All I was trying to do was to somehow ease Jerry's pain. Both my inner child and mine now. That said, after my third word *likable*, there was one more word I came up with which I thought completed little jerry's story.

Fourth Word

My (our) fourth word is very simple. Once I picked the word that I thought would make my mom love me, and then make me visible, I needed to *control* it as much as I could. In some ways, this is a one-word oxymoron.

If little jerry was going through all this trouble to get attention and love . . . it stands to reason that *likable* wasn't the final word. He had to somehow try to ensure *likable* was going to continue to get attention and hopefully result in love, which means he (I) had to keep it going somehow to ensure that third word stayed on track. That soon morphed into, *I must control being likable in every situation.* For me, *likable* was necessary to receive the attention I so desperately wanted and desired. It was found in that younger Jerry who had to sit in the chair while his friends buzzed, snipped, and chopped his locks, the older Jerry who moved his sister's furniture so he could be *likable* to her friends and roommate, plus the Jerry after the football game, and countless other situations where I had to *control* being *likable*.

In order to get and keep that attention, I needed to control my persona, my mask for the rest of the world, all day every day. *likable* was my mask. The "I'm so easygoing and things just roll off my back" mask. Or the other things I did to avoid confrontation, like not telling people what I really think or feel to avoid any possibility of conflict. Or the very worst thing in the world that could happen to me: they won't like me! My fourth word's only job is to do anything possible to not allow that to happen.

Our fourth word is a predestined letdown. Having to control *anything* all the time is like explaining what water tastes like. It's this side of impossible. Having to *control* appearing a certain way to the rest of the world through our third-word persona is no different.

Invisible → Unloved → Likable → Control →

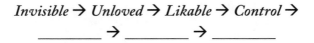

_____ → _____ → _____

The amount of time we stay in our fourth word *control* differs each time we're in it. It's as unpredictable as the word *control* itself. As long as we feel our third word has a chance of getting attention and possibly love, we'll let our fourth word keep trying to do its thing. But after sitting with my (our) fourth word, I realized if *control* did its job, then little jerry and all the Jerry's that followed would always be likable and little jerry would have no reason to be so upset. But he was. Which simply reinforced the notion that it's impossible to control anything including being likable. Which also means there had to be some sort of fallout when control ultimately fails. There was.

Fifth Word

My fifth word was a direct result of the capsizing of my fourth word.

I soon realized I was searching for a word that would follow the predestined letdown of *control*. The word *fear* came up briefly, but that seemed too dire. My gut told me the word shouldn't seem scary or terrifying. After an inordinate amount of time, I realized the word for what happens when I begin to lose control of being *likable* is *frustration*. Not with a grim connotation, but representing more of a hindrance, or better yet, disappointment at the loss of my *likable* persona.

Throughout my life, the instant somebody reacted to me "abnormally" or they just didn't respond the way I had hoped, that triggered me to bolt from *control* to *frustration*. Sometimes it took a while, like a spill creeping to the edge of the table. Other times it happened in a New York minute. It might have been because of only a teeny-tiny micro-expression seen only by me. Or, more likely, imagined by me. But in my mind, when somebody gave me a "look" that they might not be buying what I'm selling, it automatically signaled to my brain "danger . . . we're losing *control* of *likable*." Once my ego perceived it, I automatically clicked into the next gear of my story, my fifth word, *frustration*.

Invisible → *Unloved* → *Likable* → *Control* →
Frustration → _____ → _____

This isn't about showing visual *frustration*, although that may occur. This *frustration* usually happens within the confines of our internal unconscious psyche. Once we're there, it acts almost like a particle accelerator propelling us directly into our next word. Our individual, fail-safe sixth word.

Sixth Word

The "Life is about one thing" aphorism from the *City Slickers* scene still remained relevant. Then I remembered that voice from my second meditation that blurted out, "You gave your power away your whole life so other people would like you or love you." I'd already figured out I had to be *likable* to get attention and be loved. I knew the answer was in there, but where? My gut instinct was that *you gave your power away your whole life* was the missing dot. What was the connection? What did I do repeatedly to give my power away to others? I took turns sitting, leaning, or lying on each soft surface in every room. Reliving my relationships in detail. Every breakup, irritation, misstep, blunder, and disappointment.

Given where this process had gone so far, it was most likely a word. One word that sabotaged me and damaged little jerry. Something I did when *likable* wasn't working. *Let me think. I put the women I was in relationships with on a pedestal. Was that it?* Nope. Pedestal didn't work. *I let them get their way to keep the peace even though I didn't want to.* Sounded right, but again, not one word. *I usually deferred to their wants, needs, and desires in order to avoid conflict at all costs.* Defer? No, weird word. Submit, obey, passive? No. Surrender? Closer but not quite right. How about "acquiesce"? No. Way too bougie.

I stopped thinking, closed my eyes and sat quietly. Then the word sucker-punched me. *subordinate*. That was it. BAM! That's what I became in every relationship my whole life, starting with my mom. I deferred to and slid into a subordinate position to avoid conflict at all costs. I gave my power away with Mom and with other people my whole life. That's what little jerry was crying about on the park bench. His "I can't do it anymore, I'm so tired." Heck, he'd been doing *it*—having to be *likable* and *subordinate* since he was three, thirteen, twenty-three, thirty-three, forty-three . . . This poor kid. *Subordinate* became his default action when *likable* didn't work. And it never worked for any Jerry of any age. But he or we didn't know that. Nobody said, "Hey, Jerry, let that crap go. You made that story up. It never worked and it wasn't real. Just forget it." Nobody told little me. Nobody could tell him because no one knew about it. Until these dots got connected and this came to light, all the collective Jerrys were clueless about it all. No idea that that was our go-to, failsafe action when things went sideways. It made so much sense.

Invisible → Unloved → Likable → Control →
Frustration → Subordinate → _____

Seventh Word

Discovering that my go-to response when things didn't work for me was *subordinate* since I was little three-year-old Jerry was a landmark moment. That Sunday evening was the first time I understood what little jerry was carrying around. *Invisible → Unloved → Likable → Control → Frustration → Subordinate*. I was ecstatic to get it. To uncover the secret. I quietly sat with it and owned it for a while. But something bothered me. It seemed static. Too finite. When little jerry was crying on the bench, he said, "I'm so tired. I've been doing it for so long I just can't carry it anymore. Please help me." Scratching my prickly, unshaven chin, it hit me. If he was so tired and doing it for so long—decades—then the words (the story) must have been reoccurring. On a loop. That made sense. Repeating over and over like the *Groundhog Day* movie.

Sharpie in hand, I scribbled down "return," "reoccur," and then came *repeat*. That's it. The end of the story that goes back to the beginning over and over and over. The seventh word was ***repeat***. At that moment, I knew it was right. I could feel it was.

Invisible → Unloved → Likable → Control →
Frustration → Subordinate → Repeat

The Words of Your Story Go Round and Round and Round

There it was. What little jerry had been carrying around for decades. What he couldn't shake—this monstrous boulder on his tiny shoulders. I now understood his pain, sadness, and his exhaustion. But why was it so hidden? Why did it remain so buried all these decades and why couldn't the grown-up version of myself see how I was sabotaging all my relationships, especially the one with myself, all these years? Down inside the rabbit hole of dots while collecting and inspecting Jung's inner-child work, the answer dot unknowingly appeared.

The reason little jerry, Medium Jerry and Big Jerry couldn't let go of this story was because it is a thing that is buried inside our unconscious minds, unknowingly directing our lives. It drove my fear of confrontation, my poor self-esteem, and my people-pleasing persona that put everyone else in my life before me. My unconscious, made-up story that not only never worked but also kept me in a continuous loop.

A short time later, I turned my linear 7 Word Story into a circular design, because my story was anything but linear or unbending. A linear sentence has a beginning and a period at the end, while a continuous, seemingly endless reoccurring one does not.

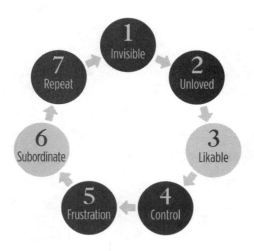

The Circular Puzzle That Is My 7 Word Story

This unconscious story which caused my unconscious actions was now brought into the light, and it changed me forever. Especially the relationship with myself. Once this all came together, I couldn't stop reliving my decades of unconscious people-pleasing behaviors. Tiny scenes from my life crept in, similar to the ones mentioned earlier. All of a sudden, I wanted to jump back in time and confront my high school girlfriend for cheating on me. For weeks I knew but didn't bring it up because I didn't know how to. When she ignored me at a party in front of all our friends I went home devastated. That turned out to be our dysfunctional, never-acknowledged "breakup" which damaged me for years. Or when my father-in-law called me an idiot at Thanksgiving dinner, then stormed off. For decades I recreated that scenario in my head where I followed him to his den and told him, "My own father never called me names, and you won't either." Of course, *likable/subordinate* Jerry forbid that from playing out. Now I know why.

I was so disappointed with myself reliving those past fears of confrontation, but afterward I realized I was purging those old regrets and the many others that came up. This was part of the new, freed self I was experiencing. Reliving those recollections I guess I could say I was unconscious, unaware, or as I eventually describe it, in a state of sleepwalking. One thing was now obvious: there was absolutely no way I was going back!

That my *likable* mask drove me to being *subordinate* was the biggest discovery imaginable for me. My past suddenly began to make sense. The insecurities, self-judgment, and people-pleasing, the pretending that I was OK with what other people wanted over what I wanted. When I explained the process for the first time and showed this wheel of discovery to a friend, he related to five of the seven immediately. It was my third and sixth words that created a disconnect for him. His persona or mask to get attention turned out to be *appease*, and that became his third word. And when frustration occurred for him, his go-to response became his sixth word, *sabotage*. Eventually, I tried it with others. Their third and sixth words were both different. The more I shared my 7 Word Story, the more it became obvious this process was more universal than I could have imagined. I had unexpectedly tapped into a shared, communal, and unconscious story.

PART II

Their 7 Words

A Deeper Dive into How Our Unconscious Words Affect Us All

Up to now, you've only experienced the words through my lens. So, before we get to your words, I think it might be helpful to understand how the 7 Words play out in people's lives every day.

I have done the 7 Words with over two hundred people to date, and there are many I have done in-depth follow-up interviews with. Some of these folks have become my clients for ongoing sessions. I have chosen a few interviews to share with you. These men and women range from their twenties to their fifties and have various third- and sixth-word combinations to give you a broad perspective on how our words unconsciously sabotage us.

These in-depth interviews came from our recorded conversations. The questions and answers were edited for time and space but not taken out of order. The answers were also edited for clarity. The openness and honesty of the interviewees is a testament to their character, bravery, and desire to purge the sabotaging ways they are now fully aware of. I think you'll find their journey interesting and informative as you begin your own journey to finding your words.

6

Interview #1: Vin

Appease / Sabotage

He was forty-nine when he first did his words. At the age of three, Vin was living in Washington, DC, on the border of Chevy Chase, Maryland, with his mom, dad, and younger sister. After college, he left the corporate tract to become a builder of luxury homes, which is what he continues to do to this day. Family, friendship, faith, and football are his world. A good cigar and a nice scotch are often how he and I unwind when we see each other. But he also makes a martini James Bond would kill for.

Vin and I met through our sons' middle school lacrosse games almost fifteen years ago, and we're now firmly entrenched in brother status. Over the years, he and I have shared divorces, engagements, broken engagements, and honorary uncle (*zio*) status with each other's kids. We speak very often, and there's nothing we don't discuss. Including our words.

Vin was the first person after me to do their words, and he's been a huge supporter of this project. He volunteered to be interviewed before I could ask. There from the start, he has seen this book and myself evolve. The discovery of his words has given him a deeper understanding and appreciation of the choices he's made so far. It has also helped him with his mom and oldest son, who also have done their words. It's been incredible to watch him not only embrace but override his 7 Words. Although we have our own language and shorthand, things came out in this interview I never knew about him.

JERRY: So, do you remember what your third and sixth words are?

VIN: How can I forget . . . *appease* and *sabotage*.

JERRY: When I first asked you about your words, before I even got to finish the question, you blurted out, "Appease." Do you remember that?

VIN: I do. It came pretty easy. Easier than the sixth word.

JERRY: So, what does *appease* mean to you in the context of Your 7 Words?

VIN: In retrospect, it's hard to say at this point, because I'm so aware of it now. Aware of the word "appease." But at the time, it was part of the habitual pattern I was in. I don't think I was conscious of it. Now that I'm aware of the word, I could define it as doing something I didn't necessarily want to do.

JERRY: We know you don't *appease* any longer, but how have things changed since you stopped appeasing?

VIN: It's been pretty profound. Very liberating. Very freeing. It's tied closely to confidence. By not appeasing, now I feel aware and in tune. And I don't trip myself up any longer. It's been a huge difference maker for me.

JERRY: So, can you remember appeasing when you were younger . . . or in your marriage? Anything you remember now about how you appeased people?

VIN: First thing that came to mind was in college. I declared engineering my major because my father was an engineer, and I thought there was an expectation I would pursue that. It wasn't for me, and I had to change my major.

JERRY: Anything you can remember in your relationships?

VIN: Yeah, right off the bat, that brings up a memory of when I graduated from college with a degree in communications. I had this huge desire to go into law enforcement and was very interested in that field. I was engaged to my soon-to-be wife, and I was so excited about the possibilities. My godfather was in the secret service; I had relatives in law enforcement. My best friend's father worked for the State Department, and everybody knew what that meant. My dad worked for the Navy. We had tons of connections living in DC and lots of avenues to chase. My fiancée told me she didn't want that for me, and just like that, I didn't pursue it. But to be honest, I had this real burning passion and desire to get [into] law enforcement, and I didn't do it because I appeased my fiancée. I went into sales.

JERRY: I did not know that. That's the quintessential definition of appeasing. This is something you were really interested in.

VIN: I didn't even let on that it was a big deal. My career and my life, my path would have been completely different.

JERRY: How about in business?

VIN: Oh man, for sure. Business-wise it resonates remarkably well. That's been some of the most significant positives of having awareness of my third and sixth words. In the past, I'd want to genuinely please every client with whatever request they had. That ultimately caused a lot of heartache and stress. If a client wanted to go in a certain direction with the project, I bent over backwards to try to satisfy them. In hindsight, I was setting myself up for failure.

JERRY: That's where the *sabotage* comes in.

VIN: Right. When it gets to *sabotage*, it's too late. It's the snowball going down the hill, just getting bigger and bigger and bigger, and there was no way to stop it.

JERRY: Yeah, we talked about this when we figured all this out with you. We labeled it "overpromise and underdeliver." That resonate?

VIN: Resonates perfectly. I didn't realize I was overpromising and underdelivering. I was doing it over and over and over. The behavior didn't change. I don't think anybody would have been able to deliver.

JERRY: This all stemmed from trying to *appease* even if you knew things weren't doable, correct?

VIN: Totally. Saying yes and giving them what they wanted to hear ultimately wasn't deliverable, and it set everybody up for failure. Set the client up for stress, me for stress, and it was all completely unattainable. It was hard to say no back then. Now, having that awareness and not appeasing, that's been the most dramatic, impactful thing that I can attribute all this to. At this point, not only do I not *appease*, but I'm very selective about what jobs we even take. I'm trusting my gut.

JERRY: Well, I guess the easy way to define *appease* is telling people what you think they want to hear, whether it's something you believe in or not.

VIN: Without a doubt. At the time, I'm wondering if in some capacity I was believing it was deliverable, even if it actually wasn't. I mean, with the benefit of hindsight, it obviously wasn't deliverable. But you know, I think that I believed the intention was genuine.

JERRY: I'm sure you did.

VIN: But yeah, I think you're right. I think if you *appease*, whether you're aware it's attainable or unattainable, it gets you in the same quandary. Sets you up with the same heartache or agitation and frustration. There might be an initial benefit to the person you're appeasing, but in the end, it doesn't work for anybody.

JERRY: Perfect way to put it. So, this goes back to the 7 Word thing. You want to *appease*, to get people to pay attention to you and like you and love you. But it doesn't work because, as you've said, it's what leads to *sabotage* for you.

VIN: Right. I think we're also doing it to avoid pain. In my case, it was not only for attention or acceptance but also to avoid any kind of fallout or disappointment.

JERRY: Great point. I think that's how you unconsciously saw it with clients. Even though your gut is saying you can't do what they're asking, instead of telling them the truth, you tell them yes, and hopefully pull it out of your hat later. And then it doesn't work. So that's where the *sabotage* slides in.

Vin: Yeah, I think that's fair. So true.

Jerry: None of us like confrontation. Especially if we're trying to avoid or trying to get something, and we are not being honest with ourselves. I wasn't honest with myself for decades. So, I get it. Well, I think we can truly say now you don't *appease* or *sabotage* anymore. That brings me back to a point during COVID when you called me and told me you're worried about sabotaging. You called and said, "I need you to talk me off the ledge. I feel like I'm going to *sabotage*." Remember that call?

Vin: Yup . . . I was on the edge of the cliff.

Jerry: I asked, "Are trying to *appease* someone?" And you said yes, there was a young couple you were thinking about appeasing.

Vin: I remember that conversation exactly.

Jerry: We talked about it. If you don't *appease*, you'll never get to *sabotage*.

Vin: Absolutely. What was significant about that situation is that I was finally becoming aware of all that in real time as it was unfolding. And I was thinking, OK, I'm on to something here. Just going to make sure and validate this and talk to you about it. I saw it before it happened, and I was catching the pattern.

Jerry: That's exactly right. I think it was the turning point for you because it clicked, and it all made sense. The words, the pattern.

Vin: I was about to do it, and I could feel it.

JERRY: You caught yourself and, if I remember correctly, you didn't *appease*. You told them the truth instead of telling them what they wanted to hear.

VIN: And it wasn't even as hard as I had thought it would be. It was liberating. Being aware of the word and then being able to change direction midstream and not be my words wasn't as hard as I thought it would be. That was a very pivotal moment.

JERRY: It absolutely was. So, in business you don't *appease/sabotage* anymore, and I don't think you're doing it in your personal life either. If you don't mind, I'd like to ask you about your engagement to a certain person.

VIN: I trust you. The scars are healed, so go for it.

JERRY: We wear our scars proudly. Let's go right for it. How did your appeasing work out for you in that relationship?

VIN: [Huge laugh] You mean how did it lead to its demise?! Let's just say the appeasing would still be going on. Followed closely by remnants of *sabotage*. It's interesting. You start establishing patterns early in the relationship. Those patterns tend to follow you throughout the relationship, and you get into that groove. It's very hard to change. We had four occasions over six years where the pattern was continuing to repeat, and I know I was appeasing. Then it got to a point where I sabotaged and broke everything off. After some period of time, we'd reconnect again. The devil-you-know kind of thing. We'd get back together with this fairytale expectation that it's going to be different. And I go back to appeasing. Then call it off again. When we got back the fourth time, we got engaged.

JERRY: That pattern of you appeasing and then sabotaging started when you were three or four, so you brought that into that relationship with you.

VIN: I know that now.

JERRY: We've never done your ex-fiancée's 7 Words. You and I have had a few deep dives on this. If our lives were on the line, and we had to place a bet, our chips would go all in that her third word is *perfect*.

VIN: I think that's pretty much spot on.

JERRY: So, looking back at the relationship, your relationship with her, you're appeasing, appeasing, appeasing. She's trying to be *perfect*, *perfect*, *perfect*. Then it all blows up, and you break it off. Then as you said, just a little bit ago, you work your way back to each other somehow. And then all of sudden you guys are back together again. But a big part of that we never talked about was her trying so hard to be *perfect*. Or putting on the mask or persona of being *perfect*.

VIN: And me having to *appease* . . .

JERRY: Exactly. You're trying to *appease* her, and her pattern is to be *perfect*. The persona of the perfect girlfriend. The perfect fiancée. Whatever. And all of a sudden, you start to think, How can this not work. This woman is "perfect . . ."

VIN: Yeah, absolutely. We've got this history. We're great together physically. We like the same things. You start fooling yourself by thinking it's really good. Then with the appeasement, you're trying not to let her down. A clear example of a six-year pattern just repeating over and over and over with multiple breaks. And at some point, one would think that you could figure that out. It wasn't until the very last one. Even after I called off the engagement, there were continued overtures by her. I'm convinced they were driven by her word *perfect*. Even if we were broken up, we were going to be the "perfect" broken-up couple who communicated. Listen, if all that wasn't an example of appeasing and [sabotaging] for over six years, I don't know what is.

JERRY: I say this often, when someone asks, "Why does she stay with him or why does he put up with her?" I say, "Look at their words." Back to you. Given your new awareness of your words, do you feel you're looking at things from a different perspective in your relationships?

VIN: For sure. I think there's a lot of non-negotiables, and there's a lot of just having that awareness of what my tendencies were and are no longer. Along with the type of person that I was attracted to in the past. It's completely different. Ties itself back to understanding my words . . . having awareness of it. Makes you feel free. Confident, independent. And going into another relationship, I would definitely treat it and myself much differently.

JERRY: It's been incredible watching this journey of yours and witnessing you crush all this. You certainly put in the work, and it shows.

VIN: I definitely became aware of it as result of what you've put together. To get awareness about patterns of behavior that affected us so profoundly for so long and not even being aware it was affecting us. Knowing something wasn't quite right, but not knowing exactly what was not right. And being able to drill it down with you has been tremendous.

JERRY: It's been a rewarding journey for sure. I've noticed quite a change even in your temperament and frustration levels.

VIN: Beyond a shadow of a doubt. It has a lot to do with this process. And it's hand-in-hand with being peaceful and living in the moment. That's all part of what you kind of laid out. You led me to meditation, which ultimately led me back to my roots in spirituality and my religion. All that ultimately affected my day-to-day level of peace and enjoyment. Not to say I don't get stressed out, but overall, I'm much more even-keeled and much less stressed.

JERRY: Everything can't run smoothly all the time. It's what we do with it when it shows up. That's all we got. Cool. Well, man, I think we covered it. We covered your whole life. I think we're done.

VIN: Whew . . . Cool! Very much appreciate this and everything, man.

JERRY: My pleasure. Your journey has been great to watch and be a part of. I appreciate the trust you placed in me. Thank you for that. Anyway, I'm going to turn off the recorder now.

Things I never knew about Vin came out in our conversation. Even though he and I share the inanest, most embarrassing and private guy stuff, I was still surprised to hear some of his thoughts as they related to his third word *appease.* It fascinated me that once he uncovered his words, incidents of how those words played out in his life suddenly became so obvious. Going into sales when he wanted to join law enforcement to appease his fiancée was eye opening. Not for the fact that he did it, because he's lived with that decision for decades. The mind-blowing fact is for the first time he truly understands *why* he did it.

The initial process of doing the words with Vin could very well have been strange, being this was all uncharted territory for us both. But the fact that we already trusted each other and could open up about anything was more important to the entire project than I could have imagined. If I hadn't had someone so willing to show vulnerability and trust, I might not have done the words with anyone else and I wouldn't be writing a follow-up to Vin's interview right now.

7

Interview #2: Joy

Perfect / Stoic

Joy was the first official interview for this book. She had grown up in a tiny town in Central Texas, and her home life was strict and driven by Christian doctrine. She was twenty-six when we first spoke. She was a technician at the holistic physician's office I frequented. It was a small, intimate place, and everyone knew of the Words and the upcoming book. Joy and I spoke while she was drawing blood or discussing various supplements. Often, I'd inquire about her busy romantic life, and she'd gladly disclose how unsatisfying it all was. She was always easy to talk to and open. She eventually became a phone client, and we spoke a number of times, having subsequent conversations about her life and her words.

We did her 7 Words and talked about how they were running her life, especially her love life. After the interview, many dots of her unsatisfying hunt for love began to connect.

JERRY: We recently did Your 7 Words. Do you remember what your third and sixth words are?

JOY: Yup! *Perfect* and *stoic*. I remember it took me a bit to figure out *perfect*.

JERRY: Did that trigger anything? Like having to be "perfect" in this or that situation?

JOY: I remember, being very young, I had to act a certain way or look a certain way just to have friends or get attention. Since way back, I think I needed to be *perfect* to be accepted.

JERRY: So, what other ways did you have to be *perfect*?

JOY: With [my mom], being *perfect* meant being religious. When it came to guys, it was *perfect* with looks. I always thought, "Well, a guy just wants a girl to be super attractive and perfect so I could get that attention," so it kind of goes both ways for different scenarios. One being the *perfect* religious girl and the other being *perfect* to get attention from people.

JERRY: Earlier you mentioned you tried to find out what a guy's vision of a "perfect girl" was. You said you tried to be that. What kind of stuff did you do to try to be what you thought they wanted?

JOY: Oh man! I did a lot . . . appearance-wise. [Laughing uncomfortably] So, my hair is brown. Naturally. I talked to a couple of guys who liked blondes. So, I changed my hair color. Then, I got tattoos . . . because, again, I thought that guys thought tattoos are attractive. I got four. Had a boob job done because guys like big boobs. [Laughs] Cosmetic stuff like lip injections—guys like big lips. I've done other stuff, thinking that's going to make me more attractive or this guy likes this and it will get his attention.

JERRY: Personally, I can't picture you as a blonde, but that's just me.

JOY: Oh gosh. No. I did that for two years, and it was definitely *not* me!

JERRY: You said something the first time we spoke that ties into your sixth word, *stoic*. You said, "I like to pretend like I have no problems." Do you remember saying that?

JOY: Mm-hmm. Yeah, I do. [Laughs]

JERRY: What did you mean by that?

JOY: I was extremely sick—bedridden. In constant pain. Went for treatments in Illinois and Indiana. Saw twenty-something doctors and pretended there was nothing wrong. Didn't want people to think I was sick. I'm used to acting like all is fine and dandy . . . putting on a good face. Even if I was struggling with something internally or emotionally.

JERRY: Being *stoic* means acting like everything is all right. When you say pretending, making it seem like you got this . . . even if you didn't. That sounds like stoicism. Does that resonate with you?

JOY: Sounds a lot like it to me, too.

JERRY: You said you were happy with work and life in general, but you haven't found a meaningful relationship yet. That's what's missing. Why do you think that hasn't happened yet?

JOY: It's partly my fault. I'm really picky; it's ridiculous. I've probably been on a hundred to a hundred and fifty dates encountering so many different kinds, looks, and personalities. It makes it hard to choose.

Just this year, two guys wanted to date me. They were both great guys, but whenever they were about to ask me, I totally withdrew. I find flaws very easily. There's the thinking there's always something better out there. I always kept my options open so that's another reason I'm single. I'm picky. I nitpick at things.

Go back and revisit Joy's last response, but this time with her third word *perfect* in mind.

Do you see how her third word *perfect* sabotages her? Her unconscious story *invisible-unloved-perfect-control-frustration-stoic-repeat* becomes easy to see when viewed through the prism of her response. She needs to be *perfect* herself and ends up picking out flaws in others because she's searching for unattainable perfection in every aspect of any potential relationship. Now, I'm not picking on Joy. Until we make the unconscious conscious, we all do it. When we see or hear it played out it becomes so obvious. If you're wondering if Joy did indeed have all those dates and has guys falling over each other to date her, the answer is absolutely yes! She's in her mid-twenties, a drop-dead stunning head-turner with a soft, charming ease about her. And movie star eyes to boot. Certainly no need to work on her attractiveness or her appeal. But we are working on *perfect* and *stoic* for her. Now, back to the regularly scheduled interview.

JERRY: You said you weren't good enough to attract a great relationship. Remember saying that?

JOY: Yup! I do. I know I said it, but it just flew out of my mouth. Sort of slipped out.

JERRY: I'm here to say your unconscious mind throws that stuff out because in some ways it wants it out on the table, especially when you're trying to figure this stuff out. A Freudian slip.

JOY: I'm so hard on myself—trying to be *perfect*. I also look for the "perfect" guy . . . maybe I'm not *perfect* enough to have someone "perfect." I don't know! I can't logically explain it.

JERRY: You're so hard on yourself trying to be *perfect* and at the same time searching for perfection from some guy. Perfection doesn't exist, and the "perfect guy" doesn't either. You said you were not good enough to attract a great relationship. Is that because you don't feel you are *perfect*?

JOY: Oh yeah, back to that self-esteem . . . the reason is probably self-esteem and insecurity.

JERRY: Because you have to be *perfect*, but you know deep down there's really no way you can be. And so that's why your "self-esteem" is taking the hit. Just to remind you what we talked about with Your 7 Words. You made up *perfect* to get attention and love from Mom and carried it to your other relationships. You're still carrying it, thinking you have to be this impossible *perfect* you made up. The game is rigged. You made up *stoic*, too. Make sense?

JOY: Yeah . . . Yes.

JERRY: Are you harder on yourself or on other people?

JOY: Definitely myself.

JERRY: So, is there any correlation between you being hard on yourself and when you're looking at someone you want to be in a relationship with?

JOY: Probably. I know the perfect guy isn't out there, but I have had experiences that are pretty close but just never worked out.

JERRY: Fair enough. During our first interview, I asked if you ever got emotional or if you ever cry.

JOY: No. it's very rare that I do. Typically, no.

JERRY: Why do you think you hold things in and keep them bottled up?

JOY: Maybe to avoid being vulnerable. I've never been good at expressing myself. And expressing how I really feel. Keeping everything bottled up is just what I've done since I was little. It's the fear of being judged, probably.

JERRY: I'm going to throw this out there. You're afraid of being judged, and it's hard expressing how you feel. Do you think that has any connection to having to be *perfect* or *stoic* or both?

JOY: Yes. Probably.

JERRY: And if they judge or disagree with you, then you won't be *perfect*. For you, it's a double whammy. Your sixth word being *stoic*, your failsafe response is "No, no, no, everything is fine." Not pull away necessarily but instead say no, nothing wrong. No problems at all. So, it's hard for you to show vulnerability.

JOY: Yup. That's right. Makes sense when you put it like that.

JERRY: Understandable given what your words are. Pretending you have no problems. Do you feel like you act like yourself in front of guys you're dating?

JOY: Driving by myself, I'll sing to the music or be goofy. With a guy, I can't do that. I've never been able to be myself. I've noticed that on my last date there were things I was about to do, then something pulled me back. I became reserved.

JERRY: Do you feel like some sort of self-judgment taking over?

JOY: Yeah . . . probably. I have the mindset that if I do that, I wonder what they're going to think of me. I don't want to do something silly and have them not like me, or turn them off.

JERRY: Do you get frustrated having to be *perfect* and *stoic*?

JOY: More like annoyed. Annoyed is a good word, or upset at myself. If I don't feel I'm *perfect*, I can go into self-hate mode, which sounds terrible.

JERRY: Is self-hate mode something you beat yourself up over?

JOY: It can make me introverted or stressed. It can make me very insecure because I'm so critical of myself. It will make me withdrawn and depressed. Fold up into myself for sure.

JERRY: How do you react when guys don't treat you like you want to be treated?

93

JOY: It makes me sad. I know I deserve something great, so whenever guys act how they act, it makes me feel a bit worthless, Like I'm someone who's not really worth getting to know and having a relationship with. When that happens, I become more self-critical. There must be something wrong with me! They just like me for my looks, and that's it. That's why dating for me can be exhausting.

JERRY: I can understand why that bothers you. And you *do* deserve something great. That seems like a good place to leave it. Thank you!

After transcribing this interview, thinking back on all our chats and flipping through my handwritten notes, my initial feelings were of sadness. Here was someone with so much to offer. So good at her job and filled with hope and light. But her unconscious story was not only driving her actions but also driving her melancholy. The best way to put it might be: if I had to choose one single manifestation of this book's subtitle *Unlock the Story Sabotaging Your Relationships*, this interview would be it. In some ways that breaks my heart. On the other hand, this kind of story is precisely the reason I wanted to share this discovery not only with Joy but with all the Joys out there looking for the golden ticket to Loveville.

I can't tell you how many people I have done the 7 Words with who felt constant disappointment in their relationships. Joy even said, "There must be something wrong with me! They just like me for my looks and that's it. That's why dating for me can be exhausting." Her word *perfect*, as you may have deduced from the interview, kept her in this perpetual I'm-not-good-enough-for-him, he's-not-perfect-enough-for-me loop. "Perfect" is an interesting self-contradiction, especially in Joy's case, because her *perfect* is nothing more than the fear of being judged. The paradox being that she does nothing but judge herself about everything.

Joy knows her words, and I can only hope they help her break the pattern of self-judgment that I see in her and many people. I wish I had more sessions with Joy. I feel like things were finally making sense for her, but we unfortunately lost touch soon after this interview. An incredibly attractive person with a sweet, kind soul, she has so much to offer. Joy, wherever you are, I hope you find peace, acceptance, and love along with your own personal inner joy!

8

Interview #3: Kevin

Special / Hide

When he was three, Kevin lived in Austin, Texas, with his mom, dad, and older brother. Religion was important in his house growing up, and his mom's massive collection of crosses isn't easy to ignore. I've known Kevin since he was in third grade—when we moved from California to Austin—and his family was incredibly kind and generous, introducing us to the entire neighborhood. We did his words when he was nineteen; he just turned twenty-four when we did this interview, and he's still wise beyond his years. Kevin has always been a charismatic guy outside his own home. Inside was another story. It seemed he was always trying hard to acquire something just out of reach. Now knowing his 7 Words, it makes total sense.

Inevitably, he'd wind up at our house to hang out with my son, his best friend. Kevin always knew how to work a room. Any room. Peers, older kids, and especially parents. A true chameleon, which ironically makes him stand out in a crowd. For middle school graduation, we threw a party at our house and my friend, ironically named Kevin, was the DJ. By the party's end, everyone was dancing to the captivating sounds of Kevin and Kevin.

During the pandemic, I reached out to him to see how he was doing living in Los Angeles. He texted back, *My parents often lack the ability to show support, so hearing it from you goes a long way.* I never realized how my unconditional acceptance of him made him feel safe all those years. After our interview, it all became very apparent.

JERRY: Tell me again what your third and sixth words are.

KEVIN: *Special* and *hide.*

JERRY: You said you've been thinking about them lately. Anything in particular?

KEVIN: I had the realization recently how much harder it is to feel *special* while hiding. After hiding for a while, it becomes harder to get back to *special.* I wanted to ask you about people's words and their dependencies on one another.

JERRY: That's an insightful observation. The best way I can explain it is that the cycle is the cycle. For you, for everybody. Your persona to be special only then reverts to hiding as your fail-safe response. Everybody has their individual cycle, which always brings them back to square one. Or word one.

KEVIN: So, whatever the third and sixth words may be, they're connected by the other words in a circular pattern.

JERRY: Exactly. Can you feel it happening when you hit those certain words?

KEVIN: When I'm getting validation, it's easy to be productive. Without validation, it's pretty much me going from bedroom to bathroom to kitchen. I beat myself up for hiding, and my reaction is to immediately go back to bed. It's not until I can break the cycle somehow that gets me out of that place of self-pity and self-loathing.

JERRY: What's the correlation between validation and *special*?

KEVIN: Validation is how one knows they're *special*. I've always depended on the people around me for my own journey to have value.

JERRY: You require validation from other people to feel *special*?

KEVIN: Validation is my channel through which I feel *special*. It's the one feeling that truly gives me joy, emotionally and spiritually.

JERRY: What does "special" or the need to be *special* mean?

KEVIN: I think "special" is to be somebody people think and speak well of. I want people to feel good over an interaction we had or something thoughtful I did for them. I want my effect to last.

JERRY: Do you have a fear of not being *special*?

KEVIN: For sure. I think the fear of not being *special* is the fear of loneliness. Everybody has that. There's nobody to make them feel *special* or unique.

JERRY: So, if you're alone, you're not *special*?

KEVIN: Well, I don't know if there's a better way to make us feel *special* than being in a loving relationship in any capacity.

JERRY: Maybe the question is, do you need others to feel *special*?

KEVIN: One hundred percent. If there was no one else on earth, there'd be nothing to feel *special* about, nobody to make me feel that way.

JERRY: Is your need to be *special* based on how other people perceive you?

KEVIN: It depends. The times I'm not at my max, I'm only going to feel good if somebody else makes me feel good about myself. Other times, I'm completely alone and crack myself up over something I said or thought and have a genuine moment of joy and self-appreciation. But that doesn't happen a lot. I'm more likely to laugh if somebody else is laughing with me.

JERRY: Some people's third word is *noticed*. Meaning they don't care if they're noticed positively or negatively, just noticed. Do you have to be *special* in a positive way?

KEVIN: I'd like to earn it. You can be the loudest one and have eyes on you or be clever and smoother in your approach. That might garner less attention, but when you earn attentiveness admirably, it's revered. That validation is more valued than just being the loudest.

JERRY: That's exactly why your word is *special* and not *noticed*. The slight nuances of our 7 Words! Can you remember how having to be *special* played out as a kid?

KEVIN: I had an incredibly difficult-to-raise older brother. It was challenging for Mom to get him to eat or sleep. I learned how to do normal, expected-of-me things, like packing my own bags for vacations, not having to wake me up for school because my brother was so much trouble. I was always doing what was expected of me.

JERRY: What they expected of you, or you just did it?

KEVIN: I just did, then it became expected of me. I built the perception for everybody around me. They didn't have to check on me. Everyone knew, Kevin's got this, isn't that awesome?

JERRY: Did you always have it?

KEVIN: As much as I needed to fake it.

JERRY: Tell me about that.

KEVIN: I watched an older brother get his every single need met. It was tough to even get an eyeball on me. He got or gets attention by being in need all the time.

JERRY: I'm sure his word is most likely *needy*. Or *weak*. *Special* seems almost the opposite of needy or weak.

KEVIN: Sounds like it.

JERRY: *Special* to you is feeling what?

KEVIN: Wanted. I always want to be that person people are thinking about even when I'm not around. From elementary school on I always wanted to be included. But I figured out that in every group there was always one outsider. Worrying that I might be the outside one was the scariest and most gut-wrenching feeling for me. So, I tried to be *special* all the time and maybe that would secure a place for me in the group and with the people in it.

JERRY: How do you go out of your way to get people to make you feel wanted?

KEVIN: By making them feel seen and understood. Helping them with something that could brighten their day. I ran into an old friend recently when I was feeling down on myself. Almost didn't stop to talk to him, but I did. He was down too but very happy to see me and that alone made me feel *special*. We only hung out for a few minutes, but it felt so great. I always want to give that feeling to other people.

JERRY: I'm understanding *special* a lot more now. What's *hide* like when *special* isn't working?

KEVIN: I remember as a kid, I would literally go *hide* in the closet or under a couch or outside. The longer it took for anybody to find me, the harder it was to come out. And the more I would get rooted to that spot. Eventually, I realized they weren't looking for me. Nobody even noticed I was gone.

JERRY: Back to the nuances of our words. With their sixth word, some people shut down, some run, others escape. Your word is *hide*, and you would literally hide. Under a couch or in a closet?

KEVIN: Exactly. I totally just remembered I did that stuff. That's crazy.

JERRY: You just unconsciously brought up that memory of the couch or the closet as a kid. How do you *hide* now as an adult?

KEVIN: Just sit around the house. If I go out, I'm only leaving with headphones. I'm not posting anything, not Facetiming or texting. And when I don't do those things, my world goes really quiet and gets small. Drives me deeper into hiding.

JERRY: Is it obvious to you you're in *hide* mode?

KEVIN: I feel myself slipping backwards in a way that hurts, realizing I haven't been eating enough, exercising, or getting enough sunshine. When I get to the point of needing maintenance, I break the habit and change trajectory.

JERRY: Can you give me some more insight into *hide* mode?

KEVIN: There's no time limit. Many times, just being stuck in it makes me more stuck. Sometimes I find a momentary wave of motivation. Something as simple as planning out my next couple minutes. I try putting one hundred percent of that fuel into the next takeoff and keep the train going.

JERRY: Does hiding feel safe for you?

KEVIN: It's a way to go through the hard stuff without anybody seeing me as less *special*. When I lose all my momentum, I go into hiding because at least it's predictable. There's no pressure. Nothing to upkeep. More safety mechanism than a compulsion. Like a harmful habit I deal with.

JERRY: If somebody sees you being less *special*, is that a negative?

KEVIN: I've found my vulnerability pushes most people away.

JERRY: Do you try to surround yourself with people who validate you?

KEVIN: Some people are only capable of a certain level of interaction, and those aren't people that are necessarily capable of making me feel *special* in a way that impacts me. I have one shot for my life to mean as much as possible.

JERRY: What is the one shot?

KEVIN: Thinking any interaction as potentially being the last. To be able to die in peace without feeling I left anything unsaid. Or undone.

JERRY: Do you feel understood?

KEVIN: Rarely. But when I do, it's with incredible depth. Like sixty percent of the time, it works every time.

JERRY: Can you be at peace if you're not in *special* and find yourself in *hide* mode?

KEVIN: If I make it to the gym on a hard day, that's a win. I don't need the external validation, because I feel like I accomplished something. There's no anger, and I don't go negative. The anger comes from not doing what I know will break the cycle.

JERRY: Sounds like anger and self-negative stuff occur when you're in *hide* mode?

KEVIN: It'll happen a few minutes at a time, beginning with the inactive portion of *hide*. Later is when I get mad at myself. Logically, I realize I could have made a turn toward productivity, but emotionally I feel myself not wanting to. Then I find myself headfirst into useless.

JERRY: In the *hide* mode, do you feel you've failed yourself somehow?

KEVIN: I feel I've failed to keep productive. I feel like I've just been in constant reshuffle mode as a lot of people spend their young twenties trying to make moves toward bigger and better things.

JERRY: What do you feel like at twenty-four that you wish you had accomplished by now?

KEVIN: I regret not making the most of the opportunities I've had. I know at the end of my life I'm going to look back and there'll probably be a clear way I could have gone that would have led to the most fruitful life.

JERRY: Okay, I could go to Costco and buy a pallet of shut-the-heck-up, but I need to say this. I was twenty-four once. A thousand years ago. You will do things or not do things you may regret. Everyone does. Make every decision in the moment the best you can and let the outcome be whatever it will be. You can only connect the dots of your life going backwards, not forwards. Okay, off my soapbox. Now, this is a no-brainer, but I'll ask anyway: who was or is easier to be with, you or your brother?

KEVIN: Oh, me for sure. I was all about love and affection all the time. From everybody. I was my grandmother's favorite grandson. She's the one who gave me the nickname "Kevin from Heaven." Then everyone started calling me that.

JERRY: Sounds like validation to me. Is there anything about *special* or *hide* that surprised you during this conversation?

KEVIN: Uncovering that buried memory of me literally hiding. While we were talking, I actually remembered specific times in my life going somewhere and hiding, waiting for people to find me.

Maybe hoping they wouldn't find me. Who knows. It was confusing then and still is. Just getting back to that place mentally was very emotional. Had me tearing up a number of times. I certainly wasn't expecting that to happen. But it did.

JERRY: A lot of people have stuff pop up when we talk about their words. It's that unconscious mind getting a chance to finally be heard. It brings back visceral memories.

KEVIN: Just realizing how *literal hide* actually is. I remember first giving you that word; I thought about me hiding as this playful, childish activity. Something like a fun game of hide-and-go-seek.

JERRY: It can be a game, but when we do it to avoid when things don't go our way, then it becomes something that holds us back. Then it drives us to repeat and invisible again. And for you back to *special*.

KEVIN: Makes sense. Like the difference between organically singing what feels good to us versus having to sing when someone points to us and says, "Sing now."

JERRY: I like that. Before we go, I wanted to say it took me a long time to figure this all out and find peace in my life. You're only twenty-four. If knowing these words can somehow save you sixty or seventy years of pain or angst, nothing would make me happier. Let's stay in touch and reach out anytime if you want to talk about your words. Or anything for that matter.

KEVIN: And if you ever need some youthful advice, I'm here for you!

JERRY: [Chuckles] Well, I may just take you up on that sometime. Thank you for being so open and honest. Much appreciated.

Talking to someone about Their 7 Words never ever gets old. Even people with the same third or sixth or the same third *and* sixth words are innately unique. I was excited to interview Kevin for many reasons, not the least being his *special* persona he shows to the world. To not put words in his mouth, I'll take his verbatim. *Validation is how one knows they're special. I've always depended on the people around me in order for my own journey to have value.* Kevin's *special* is measured internally for him. He has to feel *special* on an emotional level where others who have *special* as their third word are completely about external validation. I know some people like that and social media is inundated with them. With Kevin, I could feel his desire for acceptance by people around him and how that's what drives him. It very much reminded me of my unconscious yet overwhelming need to be *likable*. Yes, Kevin's words are different than mine, but something about his astute observations on how it all played out for him struck me. And when the interview triggered forgotten memories of him physically hiding as a child and even now, it shows me how *special* Kevin is. Not in the way he thinks he needs to be, but as an empathetic, intelligent, and loving person. As I said to him in the interview, nothing would make me happier if we could somehow save him sixty or seventy years of pain or angst by ditching his *special* persona then running off and *hide*. He's becoming more aware, and he and I are working on it.

9

Interview #4: Tara

Good / Rescue

Tara grew up in upstate New York near Rochester with her mom, older sister, and confusingly nonexistent father figures. I met Tara through a podcast in which I was the guest speaker. Tara contacted me afterwards to do her 7 Words. She then invited me to a mini-retreat at her home where I did the words for a relative, some friends, and her husband. She was fifty-three when we first did her words. Tara and I have had many sessions regarding her words *good* and *rescue* and how they've sabotaged her over the years. When we first spoke, I could tell she was tired of giving, giving, giving and having nothing left for Tara. "I've abandoned myself my entire life," she said during our first conversation. And despite the fact she was incredibly soul tired, she was so ready, eager, and willing to change. An empath in the truest sense of the word, she is one of the kindest, nicest, most loving people you could know. Not only to her dog, Lotus, or her horse, Chance, but to everyone on four legs. Or two.

JERRY: When you discovered your words *good* and *rescue* what was your reaction?

TARA: It wasn't a shock. That's why I became a massage therapist. To be loving and improve somebody's life, even in the smallest way. I believe that's what we're all here to do. It comes back to self-love.

JERRY: What are your thoughts on self-love?

TARA: Like so many of us, I came from people that didn't love themselves, and I carried their programming and projections my entire life, which altered the way I viewed myself.

JERRY: Who are we talking about?

TARA: My mom and sister. I became conditioned. With that comes the shame and the guilt they projected on me.

JERRY: How did your words affect that shame and guilt as a kid?

TARA: Being brought into the world by a narcissist, I had to be more concerned about what she was feeling than how I was doing.

JERRY: So, you were trying to be "good" to get what from her?

TARA: Attention. Hopefully love like we talked about.

JERRY: Did it work?

TARA: No. Because it absolutely never ended until the day she died. Maybe it worked as long as I was doing it. It took me eleven years after Mom died to finally stop doing it with my sister. And now that I no longer work for her, the other narcissist, I no longer give her my energy. I see it now, but it took a very long time.

JERRY: You said the magic statement: "Work for her." With the two narcissists you were looking for love and attention but only felt like it worked as long as you kept doing and doing for them. Do you feel like you were rescuing them?

TARA: Oh God, yes, yes, yes. I spent my whole life trying to emotionally and physically *rescue* them both.

JERRY: Was the love you gave them conditional, or did you know?

TARA: No, not on my end.

JERRY: But it was received conditionally?

TARA: With a narcissist, it's all conditional. It's their-way-or-no-way that really affected my confidence my entire life. Being more concerned about other people, especially [my] mom and sister. They both had a victim mentality, something I didn't realize until recently.

JERRY: You said you also married a narcissist. Was it different with him?

TARA: Keeping him big while making myself small was similar. It's what I was used to.

JERRY: That's a massive statement. The Mount Rushmore of lines for every people-pleaser in a relationship with a narcissist.

TARA: Yeah, I never even thought about that.

JERRY: The narcissist superpower is incredibly simple. To be able to suck energy from everybody else so they can power their own lives. So, being married to a narcissist felt normal to you?

TARA: It did. He was shady. He cheated on me the whole marriage. It felt just like life with my mom. Her being married, living with a different guy, getting pregnant by yet somebody else. Then my sister, jumping from boyfriend to boyfriend. Kid after kid with different fathers.

JERRY: He fit right in. Your mom even lied about who your dad was, if I remember correctly.

TARA: She first said it was my sister's dad. Then said it was some friend of the family. Even though I asked her directly, she never told me the truth. I found out who my real dad is ten years after she died.

JERRY: That's harsh. Especially to someone who feels so much. Do you think being an empath by nature served you through all this?

TARA: No. Because I would put everybody else's needs before my own. I guess I thought it was an act of pure love. But ultimately, I wasn't loving or honoring myself.

JERRY: Putting other people first, being *good*, and rescuing them, were you trying to work for their approval to get acceptance from them?

TARA: One hundred percent yes. I was seeking love the whole time.

JERRY: Did you ever get it?

TARA: Never did. Always wound up hurting my own feelings over and over. Until very recently.

JERRY: Explain your hurt feelings.

TARA: Nobody saw me for me. Didn't appreciate the love surrounding what I was doing. It hurt my feelings that they didn't see it and love me back. I felt that from everyone I tried to, I guess, *rescue*.

JERRY: What is another word for *rescue*? What you did for all these people?

TARA: [Long pause] "Save"?

JERRY: That's the word. So your job was to *rescue* or save everybody?

TARA: Yup. The same way I wanted everyone to save me. Except nobody ever did, so I always did the saving. I was a mom to my mom my entire life, and to my own detriment. Constantly saved my sister. Her kids. My sociopath nephew lived with us for years. So did my daughter's boyfriend and his brother who were both not nice people. I even rescued the guy who my mom said was my dad but wasn't. He was needy and I tried to be there for him. He hurt my feelings constantly, and I cried every time I got off the phone. My God, like a flashback of my life. No wonder I was so exhausted.

JERRY: Do you look at that differently now than you did before?

TARA: Yes. And I'm still a work in progress.

JERRY: Given what you now know about yourself, what has changed about how you relate to other people?

TARA: For the first time, I'm drawing true boundaries in my life. This is what I'm going to do and what I'm not going to do. As you've told me over and over—if you're not *good* to me, or not *good* for me, I will not be *good* to you. And I'm going to limit my time around you or cut you out of my life altogether. I know that seems harsh, but that's the new reality.

JERRY: It's not harsh but necessary for your own self-worth, acceptance, and self-sufficiency. You brought up you were always *good* even to people who weren't *good* to or for you. Did you do that your whole life before recently?

TARA: Oh, for sure. That was one of the most brilliant statements you ever told me. I was like, *what?!* What do you mean I don't have to be *good* to people who aren't *good* to me or for me? Are you fucking kidding . . . why the hell didn't someone tell me that a long time ago!

JERRY: I remember your response the first time we talked about that. It opened my eyes too. I realized that you almost felt an obligation to be *good* to everyone no matter what. What did that feel like to realize you didn't have to be *good* to everyone?

TARA: It was so freeing. I felt like, honest to God . . . are you kidding? It just went against everything I ever thought. Then it just made so much freaking common sense. That was really the clarity that has allowed me to draw boundaries in a loving, accepting way. Like I don't have to be angry at people for the way they are, but I don't have to be *good* to them either. They remain the most freeing, loving words of advice I ever got in my life.

JERRY: I'm thrilled to hear that. I think it's good advice for all of us, but for you especially, because you felt like you had to be *good*. Speaking of, this is a perfect segue. Please remind me what your mom's last words to you were before she died?

TARA: [Huge laugh] Wow, she said, "Be good."

JERRY: That still blows me away!

TARA: She hadn't spoken in twenty-four hours and then literally the last two things she said to me were, "I see angels and birds. Be good!" Since as far back as I can remember, before she hung up the phone she would say, "I love you. Be good." Every single time.

JERRY: Goosebumps. That's crazy. I just thought of something, and you tell me if I'm wrong, but "I love you, be good" . . . there's some carry-on baggage that comes with that.

TARA: You know, you're right. She used to always attach "Be good" to "I love you."

JERRY: Her subliminal or not-so-subliminal message to you was as long as you're *good*, I will love you.

TARA: Yeah, no shit! Want to hear something funny? Because her last words were, "I see angels and birds. Be good," my girls and I got dove tattoos on our sides representing the angels and birds . . . the Holy Spirit. I even wanted to get the words "Be good" tattooed under the dove, but the tattoo artist talked me out of it.

JERRY: Seriously? What did he say?

TARA: He asked me if this is something I can look at and still know what that means without writing the words. And I said yes, so I just got the dove. Thank God . . .

[Long pause]

JERRY: I'm speechless.

TARA: I literally thought we got disconnected.

JERRY: No, I'm here. I just had this insane thought. That would be like me getting a tattoo on my forearm that reminded me to "Be likable."

TARA: Exactly. After she died, I went to a jeweler and got a necklace of a dove, and on the back, I had engraved, *I see angels and birds. "Be good" Mama 7/11/11.* I wore it every day. And for nine months, I had severe panic attacks. I stopped wearing it and haven't worn it since.

JERRY: Looking back, how do you feel about all that?

TARA: It's still unfolding, how all that's connected. How my earliest programming of being *good* and to *rescue* played out. There was something that kept me from wearing that necklace. And I never really knew why. It's really more of a feeling than anything I could put into words.

JERRY: Well, you're an empath. You're all about feeling, so it's not surprising. Maybe something about that necklace and those words instinctively felt dysfunctional to you, but you didn't know exactly what.

TARA: I'm not saying the necklace was the reason I was having panic attacks, but that programming was still completely reinforced for sure.

JERRY: Let me ask you this, did you ever feel like you weren't *good*?

TARA: Never.

JERRY: Did you ever feel like you weren't *good* enough?

TARA: Oh yeah, like always!

JERRY: What is your feeling not *good* enough about?

TARA: That touches every single part of my life, that feeling of not being *good* enough. I think I'm finally to that point of having worked through a lot of this. I'm really just starting to experience what life feels like. For instance, when you asked me to do this interview a few days ago, it hit me that I don't *rescue* people anymore. It's something I used to do without thinking. Like being *good*. But they are in the past now.

JERRY: It's like your dysfunctional ex. Now he's just the narcissist you used to be married to.

TARA: Oh my God, that's so funny. Exactly like that. I still have work to do, but I'm really way further than I was.

JERRY: You're way further than you think you are.

TARA: I'm cracking my way out the shell as we speak.

JERRY: Answer this: what is your not *good* enough?

[Long pause]

TARA: That's a hard question.

JERRY: Yes . . . and no. Let me throw a word out and see how it resonates? Not *lovable* enough.

TARA: Yeah, never ever, ever would I have thought that, but yes.

JERRY: Where's that from? Where does that not-*lovable* come from?

TARA: I think the conditions put on me in order to receive love from other people.

JERRY: The conditions put on you, or the conditions *you* put on you?

TARA: Well, the conditions I abided by.

JERRY: This is really huge by the way. The conditions you abided by. You being *good* and rescuing other people to get love and attention that never worked.

TARA: You're right. As long as I would do the certain things, then I would feel loved by them.

JERRY: But it was temporary. And conditional. As long as you do, do, do more and more and more. And as long as you made them feel better.

TARA: Unfortunately, that's what I did.

JERRY: I believe you finally understand you made up you have to be *good*, you made up you have to *rescue*. It's no stretch to say you made up you're not *lovable* either. Or good enough. Can you see that?

TARA: That's exactly where I am now. Basically, if you're not *good* to me, if you're not *good* for me, I'm going to draw my boundaries. I do deserve that. And I'm *good* enough and not looking for anyone's permission anymore.

JERRY: That's gigantic. So, you are *good* enough.

TARA: Yup. I am.

JERRY: Say the words for me please . . .

TARA: I am *good* enough!

JERRY: Mic drop! End of interview.

The recorder was still rolling for this next part. P.S. I'm incredibly grateful it was.

TARA: I wanted to tell you about my experience in New York last weekend. For the first time ever, I literally felt *good* enough when I was there. I was always intimidated, didn't feel worthy enough or *good* enough or that I belonged, or any of that stuff. This time, I had such an overwhelming obvious sense of peace and living in the moment, it wasn't hard. Whether it was at a restaurant, with the people serving us, the people walking by, all these beautiful people on gigantic screens. I didn't feel like any of us were different. It truly was the first time I felt that oneness, that we are all the same. You are no better than me. We are just doing life in different ways. Your struggles are just like mine. Your stories are just different. And I never felt that way before.

JERRY: Wow! Just Wow!

TARA: I felt like I just stepped into the room brand-new, and I somehow embodied that in every way. It was pretty life-changing.

JERRY: Well, not only did you step in the room, but you also belong in the room. I'm so happy for you. My God, this is huge. I can only say incredible.

If there is one person or story that is the embodiment of how knowing your words can change your life, it is definitely Tara. She not only did her words, but she also did the work. She not only felt the pain, but walked bravely through it. Again, even with someone like Tara whom I know so incredibly well, some of what came out in her interview shocked me. I would like to thank that random tattoo artist for talking Tara out of tattooing "Be Good" under the dove. That was close. But also, an incredible reminder of the powerful unconscious message our words can wield. Long before this interview I knew she had turned the corner and was now living in function and finally letting go of her non-serving dysfunctional childhood story. I must say, out of all the people I've advised, she is by far the most open, willing, and driven client one could ask for. She came to me wanting desperately and, more importantly, willing to change her old ways. And she certainly has done that. The embodiment of how knowing your words can reshape your life. And along the way she became a ~~good~~ *great* friend.

10

Interview #5: Reba

Obedient / Pretend

Reba is from a tiny town in Lackawanna County, Pennsylvania, a few clicks north of Scranton, which I later discovered is known as the "Birthplace of First Aid." Reba doesn't heal with bandages, but she does through her work as a massage therapist. Something she is quite proud of. She was fifty-five when we did her words and is happily married. Well, now she is.

She was one of the folks I met at Tara's home retreat. They have been good friends for decades and sometimes work together. Before this interview, I had only met Reba once when I did her words at Tara's, and we spoke one other time to do a quick follow-up. Reba, like Tara, not only took her words seriously but recognized early on how they had tripped her up her entire life and led her directly to repeat the same patterns she unknowingly laid out for herself when she was young. She believes she and her mom even shared the same third word which, in some ways, made her understand her mom more but also caused a bit of a sting. She was incredibly open and easy to talk to.

JERRY: I appreciate you doing this. Do you remember your third and sixth words?

REBA: Yes, I do. *obedient* and *pretend*.

JERRY: Any thoughts or revelations on those two words?

REBA: I'm using them as a tool. I run a lot of things past them now, like when I make a decision, asking myself, are you just being *obedient*? Is this what you want to do, and does it feel good to you?

JERRY: Is that working?

REBA: It is. It opens the opportunity to do inner healing. I don't have that need to be *obedient* to anyone. It's really helped a lot. I have had a lot of opportunity recently, especially with my dad.

JERRY: You told me of your dad's narcissistic tendencies. What does having a narcissistic parent mean for you?

REBA: With a narcissist you're never going to get the love you're looking for. They're stuck in their own mirror and don't care about anybody else.

JERRY: Exactly. The narcissist extracts energy from other people to power their own lives. Has your relationship with your dad changed since you've uncovered *obedient/pretend*?

REBA: Yes, I've learned to set boundaries. Completely different dynamic. I see what you're saying about the energy thing. Something to that.

JERRY: Your *obedient* has been with you since childhood. What did that word look like to you?

REBA: Get love by being a people-pleaser.

JERRY: When you say people-pleaser, do you put *obedient* in that same category?

REBA: I think if someone's *obedient*, that's pleasing to the other person. Behaving the way they want you to.

JERRY: To what end?

REBA: Always comes down to getting their love. Thinking that's the way.

JERRY: Did it bring love?

REBA: No. I was seeking it from other people.

JERRY: Do you have siblings?

REBA: Two older sisters and a baby brother.

JERRY: Do you think any of your three other siblings' third word might be *obedient*?

REBA: [Laughs] No.

JERRY: Agreed. Our siblings can't have the same third word, or we'd cannibalize each other trying for attention. How do you think your brother and sisters get attention?

REBA: My older sister uses achievement. Two doctorate degrees, retired military as a high-ranking official at the Pentagon. Then she went to seminary school, became a pastor. Then a chaplain.

JERRY: Well, *overachiever* sounds like her third word. What about your other sister? What do you think about her word?

REBA: Service in some way. Always being the person helping everybody.

JERRY: Hers may be *helpful*. Your brother?

REBA: He was the baby and protected the girls. He didn't have the same childhood experience we did. Totally different.

JERRY: Actually, none of you had the same experience growing up. Your parents were in different life stages for all of you. If you had to guess his word?

REBA: Something like getting in trouble to get attention?

JERRY: Hard to know without asking him, but more than likely, *noticed, enough,* or *powerless*. You told me your siblings were supportive regarding your first husband. Did *obedient* play out in your first marriage?

REBA: Well, he's a grandiose narcissist. Everything was measured by me being a Good Wife. That meant being *obedient* to him and whatever he wanted.

JERRY: Tell me about that. Why did you feel you had to give in to everything he wanted?

REBA: Didn't have to, I chose to. I thought that's how I was going to get his love—by being *obedient* to all his expectations. Like always having short hair. Staying under 120 pounds. All so I could be exactly how he wanted me to look on his arm at business functions. Sexually, too. We had sex every other night the ten years we were together because he wanted to.

JERRY: How did the marriage end?

REBA: I had suspicions he cheated, but every time I brought it up, he'd gaslight me. Called me crazy, insecure. Then I found out for sure. He told me if I was so upset, I needed to be a better wife for him to give up the girlfriend and stay married. So, I became even more over-the-top *obedient* to save the marriage. We had a special-needs child, and I was petrified to be on my own taking care of my son financially. I needed my husband monetarily. I told him I'd be everything he wanted me to be if he gave up the other woman.

JERRY: What did that feel like when you decided to amp up *obedient*?

REBA: Torture. If I had any self-anything left at all, I handed it over.

JERRY: You had to be super obedient. Was that a conscious choice?

REBA: Not really, he had me so brainwashed and gaslighted I wasn't aware of much. Now I see I was in survival mode.

JERRY: Did you question what you were doing as it was happening? The gaslighting and all?

REBA: No, I was just trying to save the marriage.

JERRY: How did this all play out?

REBA: Three months later, we were in the emergency room, our son was dying, and he's outside on the phone with the girlfriend. Our son passed away that night, and my financial fears of taking care of him went with him. I was in shock. My husband wasn't showing me any love or comfort. There was no grieving together. After a week I said, "What are you doing, why are you here?" He said, "What would people think of me if I left you right now?"

JERRY: That's a true narcissist right there. What did you say?

REBA: Get the fuck out.

JERRY: Not much else to say about that . . . [Pause] Do you think your sixth word *pretend* played a part somewhere in there?

REBA: Yeah. I was pretending I was happy and all that was normal.

JERRY: How did that manifest itself?

REBA: I practiced it for so long by that point it was just automatic, the pretending to be happy and everything was great.

JERRY: Any other examples of *pretend* you could think of growing up?

REBA: I played make-believe as a child to escape the house, the beatings. I had a big fantasy life I pretended to have. I'd go outside with my stuffed animals and dolls and *pretend* I lived in a normal house. My house was not normal.

JERRY: In what way?

REBA: Mom did whatever Dad said. He said jump, she would. Never questioned him. He was always angry. We weren't allowed to make noise or play. If we were in the house, we had to sit quietly. If anybody acted like a kid, they got beaten. I wouldn't have friends over because my dad was mean. It was embarrassing. I didn't want friends to come over or spend the night. That's not normal.

JERRY: Did you ever talk about your upbringing with your friends?

REBA: No. I was pretending everything was fine.

JERRY: This may be a hard question, but do think your mom's third word may also have been *obedient*?

REBA: Absolutely. She played along with whatever Dad wanted.

JERRY: What does that bring up when you look back at all that?

REBA: I've done a whole lot of reparenting in my mind. That girl who just would do anything for love. Or feel secure, in emotional or financial ways.

JERRY: You said secure. That's an interesting word for us all. Another word for secure is safe. Did you feel safe growing up?

REBA: I guess I pretended I was.

JERRY: If you're pretending, then you're really not feeling safe, I assume.

REBA: That's a very true statement. Now that I am aware of it, if I find myself pretending, I catch myself and think, *You're not feeling safe with this person, why are you pretending to be?* I figured out being *obedient* pertained more to me having a relationship with the person, but pretending can come whether I have a personal relationship with the person or not.

JERRY: We talked about your siblings having different third words. What was it like for you growing up to be *obedient* to a mom who was also *obedient*?

REBA: Early, it was probably easy for her and me dynamic-wise. As I aged, I resented her for being *obedient*. But now I see the reason I resented it was because I was following in her footsteps.

JERRY: Explain that.

REBA: It wasn't until after my divorce that I was very angry at her for always being *obedient* to my father. I would ask her, "Why don't you leave him?" I was angry at both of us but mostly mad at myself for following in her footsteps.

JERRY: Being *obedient* to a mom whose word was also *obedient*, do you think that got attention from her?

REBA: Absolutely. She'd ask me if I had done something, I would tell her no. Later, I'd come back crying telling her I lied. I did do it. And she would hold me and tell me I don't know what I did right with you. You don't lie and always do what I ask. That was the praise I got for being *obedient*. And being the one that listened to her.

JERRY: I know our words are our words, but if you had to pick any of your siblings' words instead of your own, what would you pick?

REBA: Oh, crap. My initial thought is *overachiever*. There's something in that I admire, but I wouldn't because I know the pain she feels. Maybe because it's not as painful, probably my *helpful* sister. To be the *overachiever*, it's hard to never feel like you've done enough no matter what you've accomplished.

JERRY: That's very observant on your part. Just to clarify, your other sister can never be *helpful* enough either. That's why our third is such a trap.

REBA: Didn't think of it like that but I guess you're right.

JERRY: About the word *obedient*. Did that make you feel like you were giving your power away?

REBA: I wouldn't have seen that as a child, but I did as I got older, yes. And definitely looking at my mother from the outside, *obedient* was giving away her power.

JERRY: Did you and [your] mom being so similar cause conflict sometimes?

REBA: Not until a month before she passed away. She was so frail going through chemo. Dad wanted her to miss her cancer treatment because he had an eye doctor's appointment. I suggested letting Mom do her treatment, and I'd take him to the eye appointment and drive him back. And he blew up screaming, I needed to shut the F up and stay out of their business. Mom was crying and shaking. Then Mom started yelling at me. I went outside and cried for two hours. She was upset with me for not being *obedient* to him.

JERRY: When you think about your sisters' and brother's words, and the one you share with [your] mom, does it give you a better picture of life growing up?

REBA: It does! More of a valid picture than my made-up one. I was so busy playing make-believe and pretending all the time.

JERRY: Looks like you've come a long way regarding understanding and awareness of how you are in the world. Does that sound like a true statement to you?

REBA: Yes, thank you. I always used to think, *Oh, what does so-and-so need or what will make them happy?* Now it's about awareness, so I can have more peace and happiness in my world without being *obedient* to everybody. Finally, it's important what makes me happy.

JERRY: That's so vain of you. How dare you think of yourself!

REBA: I know.

JERRY: I'm joking.

REBA: Believe me, I heard that plenty growing up. I got made fun of because I cared about my looks. Dad used to say I was an airhead because I used my hair dryer so much.

JERRY: It's interesting that your husband had rules about your looks to make him look better.

REBA: I didn't understand anything about narcissism back then.

JERRY: None of us did. Most people still don't. So, where do you feel you are with your 7 Word Story? Has it brought anything to your life?

REBA: More awareness. I don't know if I can quantify it. It's not like you get somewhere or achieve some medal for it. It brings me to a place of awareness, and I then try to implement from there.

JERRY: Let me ask you, do you feel safe now? If so, in what way?

REBA: Yes. In my own self. I feel safe with myself. It's no longer based on other people. That realization happened to me this weekend.

JERRY: This weekend is when you finally felt safe?

REBA: It's when I realized I'm safe with myself. I was with a friend who is married to an older man. She told me she was scared that if something happened and he died, what would she have? What would she be? That sparked something in me. For the first time ever in my life, I realized my safety isn't dependent on anyone else. I'm really OK.

JERRY: Wow, that just happened two days ago. That's pretty awesome.

REBA: It is. I've had the tragedies, the fears. Had the rug pulled out from under me. Had days I wasn't sure I was ever going to be OK. Or even stay around because it was too fucking hard. So, for me to realize, hey, I'm actually OK, and I'm beginning to like me. I'm digging this now.

JERRY: I know from where you speak. Through my journey I finally figured out what self-esteem is for me. My definition of self-esteem is no matter what happens, Jerry's going to be OK.

REBA: I like it.

JERRY: That's all I needed to hear myself say. I guess feel more than anything.

REBA: That's what that conversation with my friend sparked in me.

JERRY: That's where the awareness comes in. Having the wherewithal to understand it. Feel it. Touch it. And then be OK. So, are you OK?

REBA: Yep, I am OK.

JERRY: That's awesome.

REBA: I'm a pretty great person. I just decided that. Well, not just now. But now I know it.

JERRY: I think we couldn't find a better place to end than right here.

When I asked Reba about hypothetically taking one of her siblings' words even though that's impossible, her initial thought was taking her sister's *overachiever*. She immediately caught herself and responded, "How painful that must be to never feel like you've done enough no matter what you've accomplished." Bingo!

When I think of the old, unconscious Reba, the first word that comes to mind is "pleaser." But speaking with her now, that old Reba is light-years from that dysfunctional home in that tiny Pennsylvania town she pretended was normal growing up. There was something about how Reba used her 7 Words to understand her past and at the same time, use them to free herself from her own self-proclaimed people-pleasing ways. When we first discovered her sixth word was *pretend*, she told me, "I pretended my world was a bed of roses as a child." Now that she's not pretending or being unwantedly *obedient*, the bouquet she's holding today is real. And it smells pretty good from where she's standing. It put a huge smile on my face when Reba acknowledged that no matter what, she will be OK.

Each one of us will have a combination of a third and sixth word that have driven their worlds for decades. Some, if not many, will have the same words, and we'll get to yours next. The words may be the same, but how they manifest in different people's specific embodiment of those words will be different. We all chose our words based on the micro-environment of our home growing up. What that world was like had an effect on the words we eventually chose.

Before we move on, I wanted to share with you some direct quotes from the more than two hundred people I've interviewed who not only now know their words but who wanted to share what they meant to them.

> I'm learning to be a softer person, letting my other half in more and learning not [to] be so independent. [My husband] likes to do things for me, and I'm learning to let him. I'm also allowing myself to receive gifts and, crazy as it sounds, accept compliments from people. Letting go of my thinking I have to be *self-sufficient* and *accommodate*.
>
> —Ellen | Southwestern MO
> *self-sufficient/accommodate*

As soon as I heard my words, I immediately knew this was the sort of expansion I needed. This word cycle was a creative and visual way to expose and free myself from the habitual story I had no idea existed. This "unlearning" helped me become a better version of myself and better navigate all my relationships more mindfully. Knowing my husband's words helps me understand and love him better and my daughter's words are sacred to me.

—Anita | Waco, TX
quiet/pretend

When life sends you reeling, the answers aren't always obvious. Until they are. Once I saw the circumstances and behaviors that brought me to this point, I was able to take action because I finally understood what my issues and my words were. Ultimately, this is where I always wanted to be: happy, fulfilled, and enjoying my life. For the first time, I have learned to establish boundaries from toxic individuals.

—Mike | Los Angeles, CA
overachiever/rescue

For me, knowing my words made me understand my thought processes and, more importantly, my unconscious actions and reactions I had my whole life. I am able to step back and reevaluate situations knowing that I am in control of me and not my words. The big surprise was how easy it is once you understand it.

—Izzie | Toms River, NJ
perfect/rigid

I think one of the biggest questions people ask themselves is "What's the purpose of life?" The reason we ask this is because we want to explain the unknown. That is what knowing my words has done for me. It helps explain secret actions I have taken in my life. It answers the previously unknown questions I had about my life. It now also helps me prepare for the future on how I might react to what life throws my way.

—Brian | Hardeeville, SC
overachiever/rescue

Uncovering My 7 Words took the complexity of an inner untruth and made it simple to understand. I've been able to gain a deeper understanding of myself, my emotions, and most importantly, how I process my emotional needs. It is not always easy to confront the stories we tell ourselves, but the rewards of doing so are immeasurable. I now embrace the truth and reject the false narratives that have held me back.

—Stacey | Shreveport, LA
worthwhile/rescue

Once I was aware of my words and of the games being played by my own self, I began to see things from a very different perspective. That caused me to respond differently to everything around me. It gave me a more open mind to see things for what they really are and took a lot of the guesswork out of my life. I stopped being played by myself, made changes, and started living as me.

—Paulette | Manila, Philippines
helpful/withdraw

I recently learned my words and they changed my life completely. I just had a breakup, and knowing my words has shown me that I made up a lot of stories in my head about my relationship because I was trying so hard to be *enough* and always *go along* with him. When I learned how my words kept me boxed in for years, it was easy to let go because I realized he never truly had my best interest at heart. Thank you for helping me know I am *enough*.

—Ramona | Plainfield, NJ
enough/go-along

My words made me realize I was living my life in circles, and I was going nowhere. Everything is changed. I'm happy with myself now. The excitement I was looking for was placed on the shoulders of the fantasy of a man (men) who don't exist. I recently went to a birthday dinner and was talking to someone I haven't seen in a year and a half. She told me I seemed so different. I just smiled. I didn't tell her my mask was off. My life and future is now determined by my own free will with excitement of what the future has to hold.

—Erica | Queens, NY
appease/subordinate

PART III

Your 7 Words

11

Recalling Your Early Life

If you're reading this, someone somewhere took care of you from birth through adolescence. This book focuses on that time where we created a story for our own protection that we had no idea would turn into a long-lasting unconscious narrative in our lives. For me, I certainly had no idea little jerry created my *likable* persona just as you are right now unaware of what attention-seeking persona little you came up with. You will soon become aware of the words that have been driving you all these years. The irony is that unconsciously you already know them, just as I knew mine. Time to make them conscious for you.

Feelings vs Emotions

> *"People will forget what you said, people will forget what you did, but people will never forget how you made them feel."*

This wise observation became a transformational dot in the uncovering of My 7 Words. What it correctly states is that words and actions are fleeting, but feelings have lasting power. Being incapable of rational thought as a toddler, our feelings are internalized, and our need for reassurance, love, and safety becomes our top priority. Partly because the feeling of inadequacy is a bit overwhelming, but also because we really don't understand our feelings as children. That can also be said for most adults. The 7 Words we created as small children drive our adult interpretations and "feelings," or lack thereof.

This seems like the perfect place to clarify feelings versus emotions. According to Rachel Allyn, Ph.D., "Emotions and feelings are actually two different but connected phenomena . . . Emotions are the raw data, a reaction to the present reality, whereas feelings can be diluted by stories we've created in our head based on events of the past or fears of the future—not necessarily the truth of the situation."[1]

When we aren't getting the attention we want, an emotion is triggered. That emotion provokes a *feeling* that we are somehow *invisible*. And so begins our 7 Word Story, courtesy of our toddler brain. Dr. Allyn sums it up best: "Emotions originate as sensations in the body. Feelings are influenced by our emotions but are generated from our mental thoughts."

The infant/mother relationship and our words.

The dichotomy of emotions versus feelings didn't begin in adulthood but has been with us since our first year of life, albeit on a basic level. By age three, our feelings cannot only be biased but confusing and get us stuck in often repetitive mental stories based on past events or future fears. Not getting the attention we once received, especially from Mom, and fearing we may not get it back in the future could very well trigger feelings. Our inner child is making itself known.

According to therapist and author Shari Botwin, "We grow up, we get bigger, and our brains become more logical, but that doesn't erase our thoughts, feelings, or memories from childhood . . . Most people don't realize that the effects of those memories from childhood are what drive us to make the choices that we make in adulthood."[2]

An eternal child lurks inside us as adults. Our words, and therefore this book, are predicated on little you wanting, desiring, and needing attention from Mom when you were three.

To be clear, I'm not saying on a kid's third birthday all this miraculously appears, but it does at some point inside the third year of life. Along with beginning to understand cause and effect, by the time most kids are three, there's often a younger sibling or older one diverting Mom's attention. A younger sibling guarantees Mom is back in the 24/7 baby business. Having an older sibling means PUber (Parent Uber) to and from school, sports, music lessons, extracurricular everything. Even if you're an only child, Mom has already put in three years of hard labor after the birth labor. Given everything moms or primary caregivers do, the feedings, nurturing and, according to the American Academy of Pediatrics, roughly eight thousand diaper changes per child[3], a break is unquestionably desired. By the time you, me, or any of us reach age three, Mom, or the primary caregiver (of course, some of us were raised by a grandmother, aunt or other permanent caregiver) is ready to let go a bit for survival. *Her* survival! Parents want and need us to be more independent. Not only for the child's sake but for theirs. And at three, the child wants to be a big kid. Heck, everyone is telling them they are. Everyone is telling Johnny, "You're a big boy now. Big boys don't do that." "Sally, you're a big girl. Big girls do this or don't do that." But a piece of that little person says, "Yes, I'm a big boy or big girl, but wait a second, I need my mommy. A hug. Reassurance. Love." It's an emotional push/pull. Two steps forward, one step back. Sometimes one forward, two back. Yes, we're big kids compared to us at one or two. But we're not as developed as we think we are or want to be. Little did we know back then that feelings that began at age three would linger throughout our lives.

One question I often get is, "Why Mom when it comes to our words?"

Some have said, "I have a great relationship with my mom. It's Dad that I believe I have issues with."

Or, "My dad left us when we were small, and I haven't gotten over it."

"My dad or stepdad was abusive, and he screwed me up!"

"Dad is the one I still want to please . . . "

Or maybe, "My dad was very nurturing, and I related to him more."

All those points are understandable. I was a stay-at-home dad from day one until my youngest of three was through middle school. Trust me, I'm with you. I did most of the day-to-day. I spent as much, if not more, time with my munchkins than just about every other dad we know, and I wouldn't change any of it. I completely understand how some would immediately lean into their dads as a source of self-exploration. Therapists' files are crammed with their fair share of paternal issues and problems, but I'm also aware that my ex-wife has a bond with my three kids that is impossible for me to ever have. I didn't give birth to my kids. Didn't carry them for nine months (almost nine and a half for the first one). Their mom did. The biological circuitry formed by mother and child from gestation through birth is something that can't be equaled. Human beings can't survive without the adult nurturing, care and protection that begins before birth, in utero.

A mom's relationship is not only emotional but biological. Dr. Myron Hofer, Director of Developmental Psychology at Columbia University, tells us, "The attachment bond between a mother and her child is first formed in the womb, where fetuses have been found to develop preferential responses to maternal scents and sounds that persist after birth . . . "[4] And even after birth, the bonding continues. The medical community has observed how oxytocin, known as "the bonding hormone," is released in large amounts during childbirth and in breastfeeding. It triggers a spontaneous maternal bonding in both mothers and their babies. The unconscious communication between mother and child is a personal and intimate one.

Pediatrician and psychoanalyst Donald Woods Winnicott explains that as tiny creatures, we don't understand what a reflection is. Our only mirror is what we learn from our mother:

The mother gazes at the baby in her arms, and the baby gazes at his mother's face and finds himself therein . . . provided that the mother is really looking at the unique, small, helpless being and not projecting her own expectations, fears, and plans for the child. In that case, the child would find not himself in his mother's face, but rather the mother's own projections. This child would remain without a mirror, and for the rest of his life would be seeking this mirror in vain.[5]

Attempting to please one's mother—the person who holds the key to our contentment—becomes an early obsession. What we see back from our mother's face shapes our feelings and behaviors from our earliest days. In actuality, there is no other way to judge or view ourselves other than through approving, disapproving, loving, or unaccepting looks and glances from *the* most powerful force in our universe: our mother.

Our feeling that we aren't getting the attention we need is driving us here. The raw data, as Dr. Allyn put it, was the natural process of maturation in a three-to-four-year-old, which is happening on a few different levels. What happens to us is we aren't getting the attention we used to get, and we don't know why this is all happening, and we *feel* that safety. It's there; it's just not the same as what we were used to, but we don't know that—all we know is it feels scary. At that age, do we know Mom loves us? Not logically, no. We feel it in the moment when she shows us affection via kind words or touch. But as we have discussed, our brains aren't equipped yet to make logical connections and know for certain we are loved outside those moments.

It's in this stage of our development that we as toddlers become aware of our ever-changing emotional states. As children, we see adults, especially moms, as strong, larger-than-life, in control, and ultimately the carriers of our self-esteem and need to feel loved.

The way relationship writer Dr. Steven Stosny sees it, "Competition between the drives for autonomy and connection . . . emerges in full force in toddlerhood, [which is] the first stage of development where children seem to realize how separate they are from their caretakers . . . They had previously felt a kind of merging with caregivers, which provided a sense of security and comfort. The new realization of differences stirs excitement and curiosity but also endangers the comfort and security of the merged state."[6]

When we're older, even if we're a hormone-engulfed, rebellious, moody teenager, we can know Mom loves us even if she's not sitting in the room with us holding our hand, but not during this younger growth stage. Which brings us back to the magic word at this age of our development: *attention*. When we are getting it, especially from Mom, that connection is real for us. At that age, attention is love. And love is attention. It sounds so simple. In some ways, it actually is. But simple isn't often easy. Mom has had three years of on-call duty with us. Diapers, doctors, and deprivation of many varieties. Whether we're the only child, Mom has a new baby, or our older siblings need Mom more, she wants and needs us to be more self-sufficient. Mom is most likely exhausted by this point, but that doesn't mean she doesn't love us, it just means she's not superhuman, even though it seems like it's part of the job description. All these happenings lead to a gap. We cook up the story that we are *invisible* and *unloved*, and in some ways, not good enough. And the way to fix that "problem" inside our nonlogical, emotionally driven brain is to somehow get her attention.

Sister (or Brother) from the Same Mister (or Mother)

Do you have siblings? Are they anything like you? Anything like your other siblings? Ever wonder what planet they came from, or why you just don't get them, or they you? Even as adults . . .

You're not alone. Or crazy. Every child in a family will have a different third word. Even if you have two, three, five, or nine siblings, each of you will have their own distinctive third word. The reason is rather basic: we are all competing to stand out from our competition (siblings) for our mom's/caregiver's attention. From a pragmatic sense, any of my siblings having the same third word would go against everyone's best interest. It would be like opening a new business in a strip mall. There is one vacant store out of the four, and you want to open a frozen yogurt shop. If one, two, or all three of the other stores are frozen yogurt shops, nobody wins. And this game is all about only one thing—winning Mom's attention!

Take my family as an example: Me being one of four and the oldest by twenty-seven minutes. All of us have different third words. It works something like this: At age three, my feeling was, "If only I were *likable* my mom would pay attention to me, like me, and hopefully love me." My three sisters couldn't take *likable* because it was already my word. Like when you "call" the front seat on a trip, or call "dibs" on the turkey leg on Thanksgiving (which would, of course, stand up in any court in the land). My sisters, in no particular order, chose the words *perfect, powerless* and *helpful*. All very different, all to get attention. None of those words got us the love we had hoped for.

Sibling rivalry = Nature.

Our 7 Words = Nurture.

The theory that children growing up in the same household compete for their parents' time and attention certainly wasn't invented here. It goes back to Charles Darwin and his Principle of Divergence. It is a learned behavior even though it is unconscious, as described by American psychologist Frank J. Sulloway. "This is a Darwinian story," he explains, "albeit one with a marked environmental twist. Although siblings appear to be hardwired to compete for parental favor, the specific niche in which they have grown up determines the particular strategies they adopt within their own family."[7] And sibling rivalry isn't only reserved for humans. It's commonly understood that many bird species often eject their nest mates to get more food, attention, and in some cases, to survive.

Our job is to attempt to identify with our parents while simultaneously de-identifying with our siblings. De-identification is where a sibling intentionally disassociates from other siblings for the specific purpose of remaining distinct and to stand out. Siblings will often "specialize" and develop a niche inside the family circle. Darwin contends that human siblings become more dissimilar during their maturation through differences learned and cultivated regarding family roles, strategies, and interactive behaviors. These differences separate siblings from each other. One may become the entertaining one, the empathetic one, the quiet one, the sweet one, the nurturing or the rebellious one . . . you get the idea. This happens mostly on an unconscious (our favorite word) level.

When creatures or organisms inside the same species compete against one another, it is known as *intraspecific competition*. Just like sports contests within the same school are labeled "intramural," inside each of our families our intraspecific struggles with siblings or others vying for power go on undetected. It's not quite what Darwin meant by "survival of the fittest," but we are in constant competition for the same things. Attention. Validation. And love. Hm, maybe survival is the right term after all.

A few folks wondered if one sibling saw another getting attention from Mom with their third word, wouldn't we want to switch to *their* word? If this were a logical choice, we might weigh the pros and cons of our third word versus that of our sibling's. But our unconscious isn't working on the logical; it's working on the emotional, the feelings. We're already emotionally invested in our words to try and get attention. And since we have no idea we even have these words, or that our siblings have *their* words (or, should I say, our words have us), it's hard for us to see the forest for the trees.

Dr. Sulloway notes that siblings "compete for parental favor." My point exactly. It would be impossible to compete with my sisters if two or more of us had the same third word. That would cause immediate cancellation. Sibling rivalry is more biological and preservation-oriented, and thus classified as nature.

Things may have seemed the same over the years, but actually weren't. Even if you were raised in the same house, it really wasn't the same environment. Your parents became older with each child. As did grandparents. Which meant they got more experienced with each child, but also took on more responsibilities and more fatigue. Jobs, financial situations, relationships, socioeconomic status, and physical or mental health may have also changed. Change isn't good or bad per se, it just is. Oldest siblings didn't have anyone above them to annoy or tease them. Those who came after did. The youngest sibling didn't have to help take care of or watch the other siblings; that was the eldest's job. The stages of life for all involved had much more of an influence than most of us realize. Our 7 Words are derived from our childhood environment and microenvironment and our attempts to gain attention and love. Therefore, they're considered nurture.

While we're on the subject, have you ever felt like personality-wise, you are just like one of your siblings? Can you see the different dynamics between your mom and your sibs? If you're an only child, could you sense a difference in your relationship with your mom and, let's say, your best friend and their mom? Or a close cousin and your aunt? Just something to think about as we get closer to your words.

For me, once I uncovered my words, my universe opened up in many ways. Not the least of which was concerning my family dynamics. It was like getting fitted for glasses for my hyperopia (farsightedness). For me, my family always looked fuzzy up close. Unclear at best. Or to be honest, like I was visiting the planet Why Don't I Fit. When the words all began to fall into place, it was like I was suddenly sitting on the ceiling fan over the table at Thanksgiving dinner and watching the dynamics at work. Once I discovered my siblings' words, I began to see my hazy family interactions with newfound 20/20 vision. It all made so much sense.

Think back to your holiday or family dinners. If it helps, put yourself on the ceiling fan and just observe. What do you see or hear your brother doing that he often did in those situations? Same with your sister. How did you and your parents interact? I'm pretty sure you'll have some interesting insights even before we get to your words. I can promise one thing: after your words, you won't need corrective lenses to get the clear picture.

Family (Internal) Feud: Questions to Find Yourself at Age Three

Even with all the sibling competition for parental attention, I want to clarify that I had a very safe childhood. But whether I had *safety* in childhood is the more appropriate question.

Most of us were "loved" as children. Maybe we didn't always feel it, but most of our parents tried. Like mine, most did the best they could. They gave us food, shelter, clothing—all the textbook things we need to survive so we could grow and become parents of our own.

But there are some bigger, less tangible parts of growing up that have a huge impact on our development, especially the development of our 7 Words.

Growing up, were your parents great communicators with each other? Were they safe to express their own emotions and feelings with each other? Did they have good communication skills and share their emotions and feelings with their own parents? Were your parents considerate, kind, and open toward each other when you were growing up? Did they pay attention to each other? Show consideration and caring toward each other?

Nearly every person I spoke to had issues with self-esteem as a child and then well into adulthood. Myself included. The reason for this, I believe, is that none of us felt safe being ourselves as kids. Still don't. And how our parents interacted with not only us but also each other feeds into that.

My maternal and paternal grandparents were married for over forty and fifty years respectively. My parents for over sixty years. They all stayed together until one spouse died. If I had to make a life-or-death wager, I would bet that none of them felt safe. Ever! And neither did any of their kids. They did their best, but they were all just trying to get by. They all had their own 7 Word Story unconsciously running their lives. Just as I have mine and my ex-wife has hers.

Inside Your Home Growing Up

While we're on the subject of our upbringings, I would like to dip back into the past in order to help you create your future words. It's not as painful as it may sound. The idea is to get you into a reflective state of mind, which will help you connect to your words in a few pages.

I developed a little quiz about life for you growing up. The answers aren't qualitative or quantitative but rather introspective.

149

Your 7 Words to a Happier You

The quiz will help stimulate your prefrontal cortex—an integral part of the neural network of the brain where long-term memory is stored and retrieved.

The idea is to read the following statements about your past and rate each one on a scale of 0–3. "0" is no, not at all. "1" is occasionally. "2" means fairly often. "3" is a definite yes.

Growing up . . .

- *You were allowed to show your emotions openly.*
- *You were allowed to go against the views of the family.*
- *You were given reassuring words when you did something they approved of.*
- *Supportive, constructive words were given when you did what they didn't approve of.*
- *You were given physical and verbal affection.*
- *You were allowed to color outside the lines literally and figuratively.*
- *It was OK for you to be disappointed about something.*
- *You were allowed to be sad or cry when you were upset.*
- *You were allowed to say no or disagree.*
- *You were praised for being your individualized self.*
- *Your parents told you they were proud of you.*
- *If you did something wrong, you were given guidance on what to do next time.*
- *You were told that you did a good job.*

Given the parameters of the quiz, your score would range from 0 to 39. For all you overachieving types out there, there is no winning number or highest percentile. There was, hopefully, an opportunity for you to click back into your childhood memory and emotions with a little help from your current prefrontal cortex. These questions have been developed over the years from finding the words of people of all ages, many fashioned from our conversations and placed in the form you have just read them in. That said, this was for your purposes only. To jump-start your 7 Word journey and not to in any way judge your childhood or your parents. If you shared this quiz with your siblings, they might have given different answers. But then again, they see most things differently than you already.

We all can scrutinize or dissect our childhoods, but we certainly can't change our upbringing. What we can do is understand our childhood, our relationship with our parents and the rest of the world, and end our own cycle of low self-esteem. It's too late to feel safe in the past. But not when it comes to the rest of our lives!

How Kids Perceive Love from Parents

While I was attempting to understand the oftentimes confusing perceptions of childhood, this thought came to me:

> *As children we don't blame our parents for not loving us enough—we have absolutely no logical point of reference. Instead, we instinctively and unconsciously blame ourselves for simply not being lovable enough.*

My generation and parents of the following generations have done a better job of praising and encouraging kids. Most kids and grandkids today are told they are loved. Often hourly. They're repeatedly congratulated and told they've done a great job by parents and the powers that be who are trying to overcompensate for their own childhoods of feeling unsafe. "Every kid plays and every kid gets a trophy" was created to make today's children feel safer.

Yet I don't believe kids today feel any safer. They already know that they can't just show up at school and get As on their report card. Grades must be earned. Parents certainly would never stand for every kid in their child's class making the honor roll for just showing up. Yet in sports, it's somehow OK. I believe kids understand the absurdity. They just have no power, so they go along with the program.

The "expectations" for kids have never been higher. Whether put on them by parents, grandparents, school, or themselves, many covertly and unconsciously work for the accolades and attention showered on them by doting parents and grandparents. Attention is energy. And energy is power. The pressure to get a sports scholarship, be in the top 10 percent of your class, or get into a "great" college—or all the above—is creating an entire generation of kids who feel they'll let everyone they know down if they so much as stumble or misstep for even a moment. Does that sound like safety to you?

12

Filling in Your 7 Word Story Wheel

Think of the face of a clock. Now, replace the twelve numbers with seven equally spaced circles. As we proceed, you will see how each number and word will automatically propel us to the next. This process is, of course, a completely unconscious one, and it runs our lives unless we uncover it.

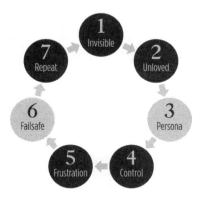

Here is the 7 Words in visual form to help create a reference point and illustrate the repetitive cycle of our own words. I've used my words as a placeholder. Just a reminder, we all have the same first, second, fourth, fifth, and seventh words, but our third and sixth words are unique to us and drive our story.

The 7 Word Story is anything but linear or unbending. As we get deeper into uncovering your words, this circular puzzle will fill in and assist you in uncovering the *why* you do what you do and help you view your unconscious actions clearly for the first time.

Your Words

By this time, you've heard all the reasons, theories, motivations, explanations, and background on how Your 7 Words came to be. Now it's time to find them. I will go through your words, including your all-important third and sixth words. You won't be answering the questions pertaining to these two words until we go through all 7. At that time, we will show you a list of words pertaining to your persona and default action words for your story. There will be a list of words for you to choose from, and your words will be chosen by you from those lists. Trust me, your words will be there.

Word #1: Invisible

At age three, we are run by our emotions with no logic anywhere in sight. We can feed ourselves, dress ourselves, and are potty-trained. Mom has put in three full years of hard labor and everyone around us wants us to be big and independent. Including and especially us.

But we're torn. We want to and try to be a big kid but look over our shoulder for Mom. But Mom's attention was being channeled elsewhere, maybe to a new sibling, older siblings or to her newfound freedom. Back to the insightful observation, "People will never forget how you made them feel." What was the feeling when all this was happening to us?

We aren't getting enough attention—i.e., love—anymore, which to our nonlogical brains means we weren't being seen. All that made us feel one thing: invisible. Our first word. Your first word.

Word #2: Unloved

Now, because you *felt invisible*, what did feeling *invisible* in turn make you feel? This goes back to cause and effect. Because you feel *invisible*, you conclude that you must be **unloved**. Your second word.

Word #3: Your Persona Word

Your third word is the lynchpin to your 7 Word Story. The framework of the made-up self, your third word is the persona that you take on because you (magic) think that if you can just be _____ (cause) that people will like you (effect). Remember, you're feeling *invisible*, which makes you feel **unloved**. You need that to change. In order to get the result you so desperately want, you need to be proactive, so you've picked a persona word that fixes the problem of not getting enough attention. Try filling in the following sentence to get your third word:

> *If I were only_____, my mom would*
> *pay attention to me. If she pays attention to me, she*
> *might like me. Then, if she likes me, she might love me.*

Word #4: Control

For the purposes of our 7 Words, *control* means specifically the control of my/your/our third word, whatever that may be. My third word, as we discussed, is *likable*. For me, I must *control* being *likable* in every situation. *likable* is my perceived, self-created outward persona. That mask I believed would get me the attention I so desperately want and desire—and ultimately love. If your word is, let's say, *noticed*, then you must be *noticed* in every situation. No pressure there, eh? That's not any more impossible than being *good* all the time. Or *giving*, *nice*, or *grown up*. Whatever your third word happens to be, the job of your fourth word is to keep that process moving at all costs. To *press* or *force* the issue in all situations. Attempting to control your third word never works, but that never stopped us.

Word #5: Frustration

As we now understand, controlling anything is this side of impossible. Having to control appearing a certain way to the rest of the world through your third word persona is no different. You are committed to controlling your third word, but eventually, control will begin to slip away. When that happens, your word *frustration* is like the silent alarm in the bank during a robbery. But your stay in *frustration* is a short-lived one. Quicker you can say, "That was quick," you are catapulted into your sixth word.

Word #6: Your Sixth Word

Your sixth word is an action word, which becomes your default when things don't go your way. It is your go-to action that you do or become, the response you always slip back into when your other words fail you and everything turns sideways. You will stay inside your sixth word for an undetermined amount of time. But when that action word fails, and it always does, you automatically click into your seventh word.

Word #7: Repeat

Just as your third word was your magical fix for love and attention, your sixth was meant to be a go-to place to regroup. Then, like a tripwire, you instantaneously *repeat* and whip back into the beginning of your story again. Back to that painful, uncomfortable, helpless place you began: *invisible.* Your 7 Word story had one mission: to get attention and love. Mission unaccomplished.

Let's Start Digging: Finding Your Third Word

Our third word is the persona we developed that becomes the daily mask we wear. It's the facade we want—need—the world to see us as. The social mask or presentation we unconsciously created with only one goal in mind—get attention and hopefully be loved. It was our attempt to manipulate our surroundings and become the accelerator or catalyst of our 7 Word Story.

The answer to one simple question will reveal your third word. If you're near a pen and paper, it might help. Now, all you need to do is fill in the blank with one of the following words.

If I were only_____, my
mom would pay attention to me,
like me, and possibly love me.

dependable	self-sufficient	grown up
enough	agreeable	nice
powerless	likable	quiet
noticed	useful	tough
easygoing	important	happy
appease	worthwhile	special
responsible	obedient	nonconformist
perform	strong	weak
independent	overachiever	needy
helpful	normal	giving
good	perfect	

The words above have been honed, refined, and curated over the past six years as I've been collecting and connecting the dots that ultimately became this project. I have put in the ten-thousand-plus hours, interviewed over two hundred people, and painstakingly honed this list into the thirty-two words above. Your word may come to you quickly as you scan the list. It happens. Study the words on the list until your word hits you. Chances are you'll instinctively know it's your word.

If you're torn between two, three, or more, write them down and repeat the question. By process of elimination (*If I were only* _____*or* _____,) pick one and move to the next. You will eventually end up with one word. Your word. Your third word. That unspoken persona you've been wearing since childhood. If you are an auditory person, it might benefit you to read the words out loud to trigger your response. Find your word and write it down.

If you aren't completely certain and considering more than one, take a few minutes to study the words in question and think about how those words *fit* your persona. For instance, *good* or *nice*? Do you believe it is required of you to be *nice* to everyone? Do you feel like you "have to be good" all the time? Always be a *good* person. Had to be *good* as a child. Even as an adult, be the *good* one. *nice* is different than *good*. *Nice* emphasizes pleasant and easy to be around while *good* is more about a deeper moral responsibility. You can be *nice* without being *good*. You can be *good* but don't have to be *nice*. If you must be both, then your word might very well be *perfect*. The distinctions may seem subtle, but the personas they create are noticeably different. Over the course of the evolution of Your 7 Words, some have told me that if they were only their brother or sister or someone else, their mom would pay attention to them and of course, their siblings aren't on the list. What they were ultimately trying to say is if they were only *enough* or *worthwhile*, then mom would. They are on the list. Others have insisted they felt like they had to be smart. That's a bit vague and not on the list. But *overachiever* is. So is *perfect* and *responsible*.

If you are still on the fence, try to think of yourself as a child. What did you have to *be* while growing up? Or even now, for that matter. Think about how people describe you to others. "Oh, she/he is so nice or good or helpful or happy." If for some reason you're still on the fence, torn between a few different words, ask someone close to you. Your partner, a sibling, or close family member. Maybe someone you've known since childhood. Have them pick from your short list that best describes you. They'll instinctively know. Why not? You've been wearing that persona for as long as you've known them.

Before we get to your sixth word, let's make sure your third word is in place. If you're confident about your word, great. Move on. If you are wavering between two or even more, stop and go back to the question.

Please, don't beat yourself up. Trust me, it will appear. Like I've been saying all along, you unconsciously already know that you wear this mask. This will be the first time in your life you're bringing it out in the open and shining a light on it. Try not to overthink it. Let the word find you. It will!

As we have spoken about often in this process, this book is not about what you need to do to rid yourself of your sabotaging ways, but about understanding your words, which open your eyes to your *why*. It's about making that conscious and turning that into why you used to do what you used to do, and that into what you no longer do. Discovering my third word *likable* answered some *why* questions for me, such as:

- *Why was I petrified of confrontation? Any confrontation?*
- *Why do I give up my power to others (people-pleasing) so I can seem like a good person?*

- *Why do I try so hard to not rock the boat?*
- *Why do I find it so hard to say no?*
- *Why is it so difficult to set boundaries for others?*

Are there any *why* questions that now knowing your third word may have triggered for you? For Tara, her question that is now answered might be, "Why was I always good to people who weren't good to me or for me"? Or Vin's word *appease* was the answer to, "Why did I always give in to others even though I know it wasn't in my best interest?" Take a moment and think how your newfound word has sabotaged you in the past. Once we get your sixth word, your entire sabotaging story will come to light.

For our 7 Word Story purposes, the third word is our persona. That social mask we as individuals present to the world. The mask we created inside our emotionally needy mind for one result only: to get attention and love. That word, our third word, was cherry-picked by us for one reason only—to get attention from our moms (or primary caregiver). That word is chosen unconsciously in an attempt to manipulate our surroundings. We act the way we trained ourselves to act and build a secret need for our created persona. Ultimately, the third word of our story becomes the accelerator. We build this "social mask" to help us create our persona. The one we will unknowingly carry with us through childhood, puberty, and adulthood.

Our personas are relegated to the people we know around us at home, in social situations, and at work. Most of us "everyday people" aren't on the radar of anyone outside our circle. Enter social media, which has as much to do with being social as reality television has to do with reality. In either case, the participant's persona or mask is there for the same reason we created ours at age three, to get attention. The only difference is that their sole purpose has become to get attention from every worldwide eyeball with access to a screen.

Built entirely on likes, "friends," connections, views, and clicks, their tower of power is predicated on the building and maintaining of their social mask.

> *"The ego, however, is not who you really are. The ego is your self-image; it is your social mask; it is the role you are playing. Your social mask thrives on approval. It wants control, and it is sustained by power, because it lives in fear."*
> **—Deepak Chopra[1]**

Movie stars aren't real. Politicians certainly aren't. Neither are reality show participants. YouTube, TikTok and Instagram personalities are anything but real. The astonishing lives filled with joy, accomplishments, pride, and superiority our Facebook friends portray online—nope. Oh, and the 7 Word Story we created as a toddler isn't real either. Never was. But we continue to judge our inner self by other people's outer facades and set ourselves up constantly to feel invisible and unloved, then try to tell the world we're _____ (whatever your third word is).

The word *persona* is derived from Latin, and it originally referred to a theatrical mask. It may also refer to a facade. Celebrities are all about facades. Maybe you know Cherilyn Sarkisian better by her showbiz persona Cher. Madonna Louise Ciccone goes by one of those names. Caryn Johnson transformed into Whoopie. David Jones became Bowie before morphing into Ziggy Stardust; and there's Stefani Joanne Angelina Germanotta, known worldwide as Lady Gaga.

We're not here to say our personas will match the enormity of these people who make careers from what their personas produce, but we created our personas at age three for the same reason they created their adult showbiz personas—to get attention.

By this point, you should have your third word locked in. If for any reason you're still teetering, take the two most like you and come back after we get your sixth word.

Finding Your Sixth Word

For me, it took an entire weekend in the same ripe sweats, scribbled pages everywhere, and a number of meditations for me to get to my third and sixth words. Thankfully, your journey will be easier, with no laundry or cleanup to do afterwards. Pulling your sabotaging sixth word out of thin air would be a one-thousand-to-one longshot, so let's not even try. But I will tell you that once you discover your sixth word, the anxiety, disruption, and havoc it has unconsciously wreaked on your relationships with others and yourself for all these years will be suddenly brought to light.

Your sixth word is an action—a *do* word—which unknowingly becomes your "coping mechanism" or "default action" when you feel like things are out of your control, or your persona is not being perceived the way you want it to. Remember, this "choice" you're making has been completely unconscious, so to help it come to the surface, I've crafted a fill-in-the-blank phrase—somewhat similar to the third word's—that will help lead you to your sixth word.

> *When things don't go my way, I don't get*
> *what I need or want, and the crap hits the fan,*
> *I _____, or I become _____.*

Pick your default action word from the list below. This word will be what you *do* or *become* when things begin to fall apart for you. Some may sound similar but are slightly nuanced actions, so pick the one that resonates with you.

settle	defensive	rescue
retreat	pretend	disappear
manic	run	subordinate
shut down	shrink	accommodate
such-it-up	victim	unavailable
escape	analyze	rigid
hide	withdraw	sabotage
f*** it	stoic	go along
defiant	give in	ignore
peacemaker	isolate	

Just like your third word, you may have nailed your sixth word easily. If so, great! Let's keep going. If not, let's find your word. Take a few that you're considering and jot them down. Take turns putting your choices into the sixth-word sentence and see which one resonates. One of them will jump out at you, and that will be your sixth word. If it helps, read your contenders aloud and see if one sets off a reaction. If you're still stuck, show your possible short list to someone who knows you well. I still believe when you see or hear it, your word will stand out in a crowd like an old friend you've known since you were three.

Another method to narrow them down is to sort them into categories:

Protection

stoic	isolate	quiet
detach	shut down	run
dissapear	rigid	defiant

Deflection

rescue	ignore	sabotage
peacemaker	manic	pretend
analyze	unavailable	

Capitulation

withdraw	give in	accommodate
subordinate	retreat	suck-it-up
shrink		

For whatever reason, my default position fell into the Capitulation category when my story unraveled. You may have gone to deflection or protection slots like Vin and Joy did in their interviews.

As an exercise, put aside your sixth word for a moment and pick one from a different category. If your word is not on this list above, pick one that feels dissimilar to yours. Now, imagine how things may have been if you had another sixth word from age three on. Strange, isn't it? If Tara's sixth word *rescue* was instead *defiant* or *manic*, I would venture to say things would be different for her. If instead of *pretend* Reba's sixth word was *withdraw* or *run*, would the way she handled things in her life be different? Absolutely. If my *subordinate* was suddenly *defiant*, would I have let my friends play pretend barber on me or given up a once-in-a-lifetime chance to hang inside the New York Giants locker room with some of my idols? Unlikely. Would I have still been sleepwalking? Without a doubt. Just with a different unconscious, go-to response.

It's difficult to explain the feeling of being inside our sixth word. For me, I somehow knew I was going against my better judgment, or as the voice in my meditation said so distinctly, *giving my power away*. Being **subordinate** was my way of confrontational avoidance. We get this strange feeling that this is something we must do to keep ourselves out of conflict. One of my interviewees is a successful corporate attorney named Paula who, when she couldn't get the attention and love she wanted by being *self-sufficient*, would eventually *withdraw*. "I just worked harder and longer. Immersed myself in whatever I was doing," she told me. Did submerging herself in her distraction du jour get Paula the attention and love she wanted? Nope. What it got her was an ongoing feeling of isolation and a return trip to *invisible*.

Our do/action sixth word became the final attempt at controlling the outcome we started out to attain with our third word. We sit in this action for an undetermined amount of time depending on what is happening around us—or, more importantly, inside us—until we realize that our mission to get attention and love has failed us. I believe we innately know the feeling. Our sixth word is more of a deflective shield against what we somehow know is a failed mission.

In some ways, your *why* questions from your third word now become about the *how*. Take a moment and fill in these blanks with your sixth word and think about your answers. It should help you understand how this all played out for you over and over.

- *How did _____ affect your romantic relationships?*
- *How did _____ leave you feeling alone and insecure?*
- *How did _____ keep you feeling not good enough?*
- *How did _____ restrict your growth?*
- *How did _____ damage your self-esteem?*
- *How did _____ close you off from expressing your true feelings?*

Putting It Together: The Third and Sixth Words

Our third word is the mask we put on for the world. Our sixth word is the blanket we pull over ourselves when that mask falls off.

At first, these words might feel both oddly strange and manipulative. Meaning, they are new in the sense that you've probably never seen them together before, but they feel eerily a part of your daily decisions. When my word *subordinate* came to me as my go-to response, it was a double-edged sword. On the one hand, it was a relief to finally understand why I was doing the things I was doing for most of my life. But it also infuriated me knowing that I played second fiddle to this word that handcuffed me for all those years.

If we look at it objectively, which I now do, our 7 Word Story is dysfunctional by nature. The fact that we had no idea doesn't change this. By understanding our 7 Word Story and, more importantly, not being run by it, we're moving from a dysfunctional existence to a functional one.

Because dysfunction ran us for so long, it became "normal," which is why function may seem strange or uncomfortable at first. It may even seem like something is off or missing. What's missing is that attachment to outcomes that have plagued us for our entire adult life. In our *new normal*, away from our made-up story, we are not quite as "involved" as we once were. That may feel like being the lone sober person at a party. Our exchanges are fewer because we've limited ourselves to mostly functional interactions. In other words, we're not clinging to dysfunctional orbits based on our made-up story.

My world now doesn't revolve around having to be likable, which means never getting sucked into my old *subordinate*. That alone changed every relationship in my life. I no longer see every interaction as a referendum on whether I'll be approved of or not. Just think how much more energy you could have if you didn't have to waste it on trying to control that persona.

That opportunity is right in front of you. Yes, these words have always seemed strangely familiar to you on an unconscious level, but now, in conscious form, you can no longer unknow them. That's a good thing, because only in this state can we make changes to what once undermined and sabotaged the relationships in our lives, especially the one with the person we undercut the most: ourselves.

13

Make the Unconscious Conscious

The Power of Meditation

While finessing this section, I sat at my computer and stared. I had a wake-up shower, my coffee, and a quiet office, but what I didn't have was a simple, succinct way to sum up what disengaging from my made-up story felt like. Thinking begets overthinking, and that helped like a weighted vest in a swim race. So, it was time to transfer from the desk chair to the meditation chair.

Using quick breaths, then slowing them down, in my mind repeating *let* on the incoming breaths and *go* on the outgoing, I felt my brain eventually clear up like a shaken Etch A Sketch. Some unknown amount of time later, something popped in from the nothingness. A word. *Free.* Followed immediately by a slight energy surge for emphasis. That was it. The feeling. Finally, after all the searching, anxiety, panic attacks, tears, introspections, analyzing, overanalyzing, overthinking, research, and dot connecting . . . the switch flipped. I was now free.

Free from sleepwalking. Free from my unconscious words driving my behavior. Free from the persona I was secretly hiding behind. Free from wasting valuable energy trying to win over other people.

Free to feel things in the moment and no attachment to outcome. Free from judging my insides by other people's outsides. Free from the need to have everyone accept me. Free to value my own time.

This led to possibly the biggest shackles that were shed—my other four-letter word that followed me for my entire life: *fear*. Now the *fear* I carried forever that I was somehow not good enough was gone. Finally fear-free!

I meditate because I can't hear anything over all that thinking. Yes, thinking. Our thinking is the only real noise going on inside our head. Sure, there's the sounds we hear in our homes, office, car or from the outside and immediately surrounding us, but that's sound. Not noise. The way to connect to our emotional right brain is through that silent portal where our ego can't penetrate because there's no thinking to cling to.

Now that you know your words, I would like to challenge you to find some silence. Stop *doing* all the time. When you're out in the world and there's a moment, take a break. Create a lull in the action and try not to reach for the adult pacifier disguised as your smartphone. If you're waiting in line or sitting at the doctor's office, stop and observe. Not the people around you, but the *you* around you. Check what you're overthinking. Slow yourself down and just *be*. You'll soon notice that you're most likely the only person in your sight line who is not eye-deep in a zombie screen glued to their hand. You can see quiet as a waste of your time if you like, but if you connect to your quiet mind more, you'll begin to see it as your time to recharge and *un*think. Give it a try. Your heart rate, lowered anxiety level and your mind will thank you.

When my ex-wife was pregnant with our second, we bought our first home together in a cute, hilly gem of a neighborhood in West Los Angeles. The house was a stretch financially and an outright mess physically. The realtor's promo sheet called it, "The Cheapest House in Cheviot Hills." It should have added: *and the ugliest. Nonetheless, we beat out five other over-asking price bidders and took on the challenge. We met a "handyman" who could do everything. I've always been a decent do-it-yourself guy, but this project was overwhelming.

With a name that seemed to incorporate half the alphabet, our new one-man building machine simply went by Mr. George. He was a soft-spoken Iranian man with a long, silver-white ponytail that reached his lower back, which gave his already peaceful demeanor more spirit cred. Together, he and I rebuilt the garage, took out load-bearing walls, belly-crawled under the pier and beam foundation of the 1928 house repairing plumbing and wiring, replaced all the windows, and completed countless other undertakings.

There was a TV show at the time called *This Old House*. In his case, *This Old Soul* would have been appropriate. One day, Mr. George and I were discussing spirituality and my futile efforts at meditation popped up. "Sometimes I meditate at red lights," he told me. Shut the newly painted front door!

I can't even meditate in an isolation chamber, was my thought. Impossible. Cut to almost two decades later and a few years into my meditation practice, I was stopped at a red light in Dallas. I wasn't thinking about awareness, my words, or anything for that matter. I spontaneously launched into meditation. Eyes focused, breaths opening and closing. The light lasted ninety seconds or so, and then I went back to driving. Suddenly, Mr. George popped into my consciousness, and I could almost feel his presence. He had taught me how to remove walls, add a header, and replace windows. Ironically, helping us transform the *ugliest* house in the neighborhood into a charming stucco oasis across from the neighborhood's Rancho Park Golf Course was the last house he worked on. My very pregnant wife and I went to his funeral just two months later.

I used to think yellow lights meant *slow down*. He taught me red lights could have the same effect. Thanks, Mr. George. Until our energies meet again!

If you can find a way to meditate, I highly recommend giving it a few minutes. In the meantime, try walking (phone in your pocket), yoga, or writing in a journal. Or go to a $1.09 dollar store and buy a coloring book, crayons or pencils. None of these are quite like the peace of meditation, but we have to start quiet time somewhere. Then you can go right back to overthinking as usual. John Lennon said it best, "All we are saying, is give peace a chance."[1]

Confrontation

There is a built-in override that may be a key component to not only sabotaging our relationships with others, but our relationships with ourselves as well. In my opinion, it's a precursor to something most of us suffer from: low self-esteem. This manifests itself in a total fear of confrontation, fear of even the slightest threat to our emotional state. I constantly lived in fear that I'd somehow find myself in a "confrontation"—anything that may whatsoever resemble any sort of disagreement or variance from the status quo. Not even a tiny hiccup. I had to maintain a certain "normalcy," and that usually meant me acquiescing to avoid a disagreement.

Oftentimes when we tell someone else about a dispute or squabble we're having, we're looking for them to be on our side. After all, we take their side all the time. But when it comes to doing something about the dispute at hand, the bravado has its limits. Following is a fictitious conversation between fictitious friends that very well could have happened to any of us at any time:

MARYANN: Are you serious? You shouldn't even have to think twice about it. You have to say something to this guy. Lay it on the table.

TAM: Really? Think so?

MARYANN: Absolutely.

TAM: So, you would tell him that face-to-face?

MARYANN: If I were a different person . . . sure.

Like Maryann above, I'd often wished to be a different person. Until discovering my words and the *why* behind them, confrontation petrified me for most of my life. A totally unconscious thing but a "thing" nonetheless. Confrontation made me feel uncomfortable and extremely vulnerable.

Let's take a moment to clarify confrontation. According to the *Oxford Learner's Dictionary*, confrontation is "a situation in which there is anger between people or groups who disagree because they have different opinions."[2] That makes sense if we're talking about the word the way most of us see it. Like confronting an enemy, opponent, rival, or anyone trying to exert force over us. But I'm talking about being uncomfortable with perceived opposition regarding everyday situations that arise mostly in work, personal, family and romantic relationships. For some of my interviewees, being uncomfortable with confrontation was justified by telling me, "I just want to keep the peace," or, "I don't want to upset others." "It's easier to ignore it," another said.

For me, avoiding confrontation occurred because of my fear that people might not like me. Then my sixth word *subordinate* came along, which told me to not rock the boat. Vin went to *sabotage* mode, so the boat wouldn't sway for him. That left both of us with no safe way to have a disagreement or voice our true opinions, which would mean having our personas be put into question. For those reasons, I avoided conflict at all costs. Unless, of course, someone backed me into a corner with no way out—then I came out swinging. It didn't happen often because I rarely put myself in those positions. But when it did occur, my Italian alter ego Jersey Jerry surfaced.

That's what happened the night my former penguin told me about the upcoming Belize trip. My fight-or-flight response took over the show. I felt vulnerable and exposed. My very existence seemed threatened as I paced back and forth across the room to the rhythm of my pounding heartbeat. It was a feeling that I had no control over and felt very unsafe in. And when it passed, I felt embarrassed and completely out of sorts. Soon after I found myself back in *subordinate*.

Most of us—my former unconscious self included—were brought up under the false assumption that telling someone we disagree with them or calling them out on something we find offensive or out of line is wrong and unhealthy, when the opposite is true. In fact, it's one of the healthier things we can do for ourselves and the relationships we are in.

If that's the case, then why are 99.525 percent of us afraid of "confrontation"? Easy. In a nutshell, we don't feel safe! There's even a swanky scientific name for it: conflict anxiety disorder. A fancy term for not feeling safe because we're afraid people might not like or love us. Or think we're not *good, nice, likable, enough, self-sufficient, happy,* etc. Now, I know what you're thinking—strange logic to go through life with. Well, logic has absolutely zero to do with it as this book has reiterated again and again.

Ellie, a woman I was advising whose third word is *appease*, had been seeing a man for over six months. "I really, really liked him" is how she put it. He called her whenever he felt like it and she always made herself available. She confessed to me her frustration regarding his same-day date invitations and his constant inability to keep promises. I suggested Ellie ask him a simple question: "Do you want to be in a relationship with me?" If his answer was yes, they could figure it out together. If no, then she would know what they truly were. She couldn't do it. She refused to ask the question and told me, "If I speak my mind, I'm automatically a bitch." Obviously, programming played into her decision. She was afraid that he would think she was giving him an ultimatum, and that went counter to her *appease* persona. I tried to get her to see it for what it was: truth-seeking. But her fear of his answer drove her to do nothing. In actuality, her fear was of him saying anything that might be construed as confrontational. Him saying no would fall under that category. He broke up with her a few weeks later. Actually, that's almost true. Apparently he was afraid of confrontation as well, so he just stopped calling.

We don't ask for what we want because we're afraid we won't get it, which only guarantees we won't get it.

The fix-it communities have all sorts of important-sounding words they attribute to the reasons we fear conflict or confrontation, such as *allodoxaphobia* (the fear of opinions), *angrophobia* (the fear of anger or becoming angered), and *rhabdophobia* (the fear of being severely punished or criticized). Of fear of confrontation it's been suggested, "No matter who you have to confront, always remember that no one has the authority to intimidate you or make you feel less worthy of respect."[3] Now, this advice is an attempt to get us to left-brain our way to happiness, self-esteem, and a more rewarding way of life. As I have learned through decades of well-meaning self-help advice like this, the problem itself is *not* a logical left-brained issue but an emotional right-brain story running our life until we identify it. That's the only way it can be understood and ultimately dismantled, giving us the freedom and power to let go of our sabotaging *why*.

Does fear of confrontation resonate with you? Can you think of experiences or relationships that froze you in your tracks or put you in an inferior place with someone?

Only on Television

When we think of confrontation, most of us picture yelling, screaming, and people toe-to-toe on the verge of physical abuse. We imagine confrontation leading to the "inevitable" anger that follows, and we fear confrontation because we don't want to get angry, and we definitely don't want someone angry at us. We can thank movies and television for those misconceptions.

In a cast interview for the show *Curb Your Enthusiasm*, actor Jeff Garlin remembers being asked by a wardrobe person, "Why can't everyone [in the show] get along?", to which he remembers show creator Larry David replying, "Because conflict creates comedy . . . We're getting along when you don't see us on camera; those are all nice, warm moments."[4] Those "conflicts" we see on sitcoms are extremely exaggerated for comedic purposes. On TV the more neurotic the character, the more conflict around every corner. Like our 7 Word Story, a storyline on TV isn't real either.

News, talk shows, and social media have adopted confrontation as a form of entertainment. More like *angertertainment*. Sports talk shows now have a protagonist and antagonist going toe-to-toe to manufacture drama through artificial conflict. If a "reality" show had contestants who all got along, it would never make it to air. We love watching others in conflict but hate it for ourselves.

Here are some actual fears of confrontation we as non-reality-show participants face. If you have ever changed a hairstylist, barber, nail person, mechanic, chiropractor or any other service for that matter, chances are you've "ghosted" or have been ghosted by someone. If you aren't familiar with the colloquial term, "ghosting" is used to describe a situation where we or someone else abruptly ceases all contact with another person, friend, or business with no explanation given.

Or say we've been using the same hair person for months or years and one day they cut too much off. Or the color just wasn't right, or they just missed the mark. Perhaps a family member suggested someone closer to our home or work who was less expensive, or their schedule was more flexible. Maybe we don't want to hear the same stories about their spouse, boss, kids, parents, or their inane political rants any longer. It happens. Whatever it is, do we tell our hair person they cut too much off last time? Fess up that we don't want to talk politics? Or that we need someone with a more flexible schedule? Do we tell the person we had a few dates with they might drink too much? Are too religious? Not religious enough? That we're not compatible physically? Do we bring any of these up and possibly find a solution? Chances are *no*. They just never hear from us again. Or we never hear from them. It may have been something that could have been rectified with a conversation. Doesn't matter. It's fear of confrontation.

Think of someone you don't talk to anymore. Was there some "blow up" that ended in a parting of the ways? Any words exchanged or farewell? Unlikely. Often, there was no inkling there even was any sort of problem to begin with. No big "chat." No airing of grievances, powwow, or intervention. No mafia "sit-down." Chances are we had a reason in our head or they had one in theirs which caused the drop. But no discussion. Why is that? Because most of the time it's much easier to flee, to exit stage left, than it is to even face the possibility we might *confront* another person, and that person get angry at us. Being upfront and honest with someone or them with us can often feel like a confrontation, and someone saying they disagree with us can directly lead us to not feeling safe. For both parties, the status quo must be kept and any possible outside influence threatening either person's 7 Word Story will be dodged, ducked or immediately sidestepped. Trust me, we're not feeling safe, thanks to our words.

During my two-decade marriage I rarely had a conflict with my now ex-wife. Did we ever have a disagreement? A few. How about an argument? Kind of. Whether Bill Clinton should have been impeached for lying about sex under oath comes to mind. Until the marriage began to implode, that was pretty much it.

James, early thirties—who was mid-divorce when we did his 7 Words—put it best when I asked about his recent breakup. "It had more to do with the ten thousand fights we never had." For me, my "anger" was reserved for marital-therapy sessions and a few divorce-decree negotiations with mediators present. Those were limited to good old Jersey Jerry fight-or-flight, back-against-the-wall, fear-running-the-show eruptions. By that point, the inoperative marriage was doomed. That didn't change the fact that I still hated conflict. In any form. Even if the person obviously had it coming. When the possibility of a conflict began to emerge, primeval forces overtook me. I had a visceral reaction start in my stomach, creep into my chest, and put up residence in my throat. Looking back, I never had a conscious thought that I shouldn't stand up for myself, or that I should let her have her way to avoid conflict. It was almost like a fail-safe sensor was secretly activated. One that said, "Warning, warning . . . do not engage, leave it alone or it will detonate, and you will have no chance of being loved." Even if I was furious at something she said or did, the silent alarm sounded. Confrontation avoided. She never knew. Nor cared. Unlike me, who cared but wasn't safe enough to stand my ground and call her out. I had no idea how to functionally stand up for myself. How could I? I didn't feel safe with my emotions. So, my passive-aggressive third finger was emphatically flipped like a dull, rusting switchblade seen only by me.

Looking back on years of pacing back and forth in Argument's waiting room, it seems like I was another person. My ex-wife's part in all this has absolutely nothing to do with it. It was my life. My fear of confrontation. My lack of feeling safe. My words creating my made-up story. The issue was all about safety. I know I'm not alone on this front. In fact, nearly everyone I have interviewed to this point has issues with confrontation. This amazed me early on. Turns out, it's impossible to feel safe inside our 7 Word Story. We are so comfortably ensconced in our words and our attachment to the outcome of attention/love it becomes too risky to express our feelings, emotions or desires.

But here's the great news about all this. Once we have shed our unconscious story, no matter what our words are, we're not attached to any outcome. I no longer have to be *likable*, so there's no more *subordinate*. And your fear of how others will somehow react to your truth will, like my behind-the-back finger flip, become a thing of the past.

Don't expect. Be direct.

> *Peace is not the absence of conflict, but the*
> *ability to cope with conflict by peaceful means.*
> —**Ronald Reagan**[5]

So why don't couples, family members, friends, and coworkers just ask for what they want? Most of the time, it's because if we ask for what we want, and the other person says no or doesn't acknowledge our request, then what? Asking or opening ourselves up to someone about what we're feeling, what we need or want, puts us in a vulnerable position.

For most, vulnerability ranks just behind oral surgery and giving the keynote speech naked at a clown convention. We are petrified of feeling vulnerable and view that unknown outcome as confrontational. It's easier to hope the person magically figures out what our expectation is than for us to be direct with them. In many ways, expecting others to act or react to our unverbalized thoughts is an adult form of magic-think.

Full disclosure: During final edits on this book, I was asked to find examples of vulnerability and confrontation avoidance in couples. After some internal debate, I decided to get personal. Really personal. Okay, I'm just going to say it: I faked an orgasm with my wife. Why? Because I didn't want to have a conversation with her about our nearly nonexistent sex life. It had been months since we were intimate, and maybe she felt obligated, or who knows what, but one night I got the unspoken high sign that my dry spell may be over, and we began to make love. In retrospect, this is where my adult magic-think brain screwed me over—pardon the pun. I was thrilled she got my hints, the telepathic messages I was sending about sex and how important it is in a committed relationship. *Finally!* My euphoria was short-lived. At some point along the way I got the intense feeling "it" was taking too long for her. In my mind she was watching the clock. (I have no proof, but I do know she wasn't looking at me.) I remember what I was thinking as if it were yesterday. "This is not making love. This isn't enjoyable at all. What am I doing? Cut your losses, dude." That's when I faked my escape. My acting certainly wasn't Oscar-worthy, but I didn't care. She seemed to care even less. The agony was over without the ecstasy. I never spoke about it before and now it's in print for the world to read. I guess I've learned to be more vulnerable. But that's not the point. At that time, I was scared of vulnerability, but even more terrified of having the real conversation about our intimacy issues or lack thereof.

Even as adults, magic-think is part of our unconscious self-attempt to control given situations. An unverbalized ploy to get to an outcome we're attached to or an expectation we're afraid to verbalize. The famous adage "Expectation is the root of all heartache" sums it up best.

A couple I know exceptionally well were going through some ongoing marital issues and found themselves in marriage counseling. After their weekly visit, they would often continue their session in the car on the way home. One particular night after a pretty emotional session, one of them blurted out at a red light, "We're married, you should know what I'm thinking!" I'll repeat it for maximum impact: *We're married . . . you should know what I'm thinking!* Can someone say setup? Not the worst thing anyone ever said to their partner, not by a long shot. But it did give the other spouse a better picture of why they often felt like married strangers.

This sort of thinking is much more common in relationships than you would think. The only thing this couple did that most others don't is saying it out loud. For most of us, we *hope* and *pray* our partners can hear what we're thinking so we don't have to literally put it out there. Then we avoid the possibility of encountering that nasty C word—confrontation.

I know your words are consciously new to you, but this might be a great time to stop and think about your third and sixth words and how they have tripped you up in the past. Is there an example or two you can think of where your words have kept you from speaking your mind with your partner or family member? Were you afraid of telling them you're not thrilled about how they make the bed (or not make the bed)? Load the dishwasher? Keep you waiting constantly? Maybe you keep waiting for them to acknowledge what you do for them or the family. It will most likely tie back to your words. Take a moment.

Here is a personal example: Throughout every previous relationship, I wanted to be acknowledged by my partner when I did something for them. Or us. Whenever it snowed or our cars were iced over, I would get out fifteen minutes early and clear my wife's car after I did mine. If you've never lived in a place with snow, trust me, it's a royal PIA. Yes, I wanted to do something nice for her, but deep down, I also wanted her to acknowledge and appreciate it. Appreciate me. Years of car clearing, and it never once got a mention. I never brought it up because I didn't know how she would react, so I kept scraping year after brisk, wet year. Thankfully, now I'm aware how attached to the outcome of being *likable* I was and how petrified I was to ask her directly to occasionally acknowledge a good deed. I didn't know what she would say, so I never asked. Fear of confrontation? Guilty as charged. I think deep down I just expected her to someday notice so I wouldn't have to say anything. Are there any expectations you can think of in your relationship? Something to contemplate.

Truth be told, most of us have great, open, and direct conversations with our partners and others in our lives. We lay out what we want, need, and desire to make us feel loved and appreciated, and we tell them what we believe will go a long way to making our relationship with them much more trusting, loving, and less scary for both involved. The only problem is that we've had those conversations with them in our own head. We don't feel safe enough to have them directly with that person. Maybe passive-aggressively, but out loud? *No* way. So, instead we revert back to the made-up inner untruth of our unconscious story.

Speaking of our story, think about your own third and sixth words. They're still new to you logically, but emotionally, you three go way back. Think about a time or two where you gave to others but felt you didn't get enough back. Maybe it happened today. I'll give you a moment . . .

Did any of those situations feel like people-pleasing? Looking back, how much did your words play a part in those situations?

Please Don't Be a People-Pleaser (Pretty Please?)

People-pleaser is a catch phrase that permeates therapy sessions and is discussed ad nauseum in the pop-psych universe, yet many continue putting others first. The *why* they do it is because they unconsciously believe they need to adhere to their made-up persona or mask of their words to get attention and love. All too often, what people-pleasers inadvertently attract instead are narcissists. Truth be told, narcissists themselves will never, ever be the pleasers. They will always jump at the chance to be the man or woman the pleaser pleases. This is a great example of how our words often unintentionally play out in our relationships with others and especially ourselves. As a recovering people-pleaser myself, it seems so crazy clear now.

After searching "How to stop being a people-pleaser," the results were downright unsurprising. Every clichéd platitude we've heard for decades like, "Be true to yourself." "Listen to your inner voice." "Accept yourself." "Try positive talk." (Insert eye roll here) "Become self-aware." And my favorite: what you <u>should</u> do . . . "Make yourself happy." Seriously? What a no-brainer. If we could just say "Abracadabra!" and suddenly make ourselves instantly happy, everyone would jump at the opportunity. Again, all left-brain logical statements or "solutions" to a right-brain, emotional issue. Which is why they don't, can't, and won't work.

While we're on the subject of pleasing, do you say "Sorry" often? For things you have absolutely no reason to be sorry for? Like when someone bumps into you, and you respond with, "Sorry," or when someone tells you they're sick or having a bad day and you respond with, "I'm so sorry." How about, "I'm sorry, I have to use the restroom." You just apologized for having a necessary bodily experience. It's a great litmus test for your possible people-pleaser made-up words. It is a backdoor way to avoid possible conflict, and as we have already spoken about, fear of confrontation occurs because locked inside our story we're vulnerable. We don't feel safe!

When my kids were, *like,* younger, the word *like* drove me, *like,* insane. My lecturing on the relevance or irrelevance of that word fell on deaf ears. In the car one day, the word *like* was used one time too many and the next time it hit my eardrum I blurted, "Bowling ball!" After the third time one of my kids asked, "Why do you keep saying bowling ball, Dad?"

"'Bowling ball' belongs in that sentence as much as 'like' does," was my response. Synchronized eye rolls followed.

After that, whenever "like" came out, "bowling ball" followed. Soon, my kids started bowling-balling each other and then their friends. Then their friends began to say it too. It made them stop and think about the habit, which eventually changed their behavior. Same thing with our words and the actions they cause. Just as my kids listening to their friends and peers randomly insert a superfluous expression where it doesn't belong, our sabotaging words often drive us to unnecessary actions. In this case, robotically inserting "Sorry."

The next time you blurt out that "S" word think about why you said it. Most often it's used as a filler word putting us in a secondary, submissive, or inferior place. We are already in the subservient position because we are beholden to our made-up 7 Words. The unnecessary "Sorry" also places the recipient in an authority position they have no reason to be in and that makes them uneasy. Like saying "Sorry" when someone dies. Unless you actually killed the person in question, keep the sorry in your pocket. Try something neutral. "My condolences" works, so does, "She/he will be missed." Instead of, "I'm sorry, I have to use the restroom," how about a statement of fact like, "I'm going to the restroom," or "I'll be back in a few minutes." If someone is sick or having a bad day, instead of, "Oh, I'm so sorry," how about, "Hope you're feeling better," or "Hang in there." Or something wild and crazy like, "Can I help?" You'll be doing yourself and the other person a favor. Back to why do we do it? People-pleasing comes to mind.

People-pleasing stems from fear we're not good enough.

People-pleasing is us trying to get others to like us because we don't feel secure and safe inside ourselves. Do I believe we can stop ourselves from people-pleasing by being intentional about it and focusing on being aware of our people-pleasing ways? Sure. Kinda. But that's an awful lot like solving our self-esteem or other self-help issues using our left-brain logic. We can't just override our people-pleasing ways.

Here's what we *can* do: break away from the made-up story we've been carrying around all those years. That's it. Once I stopped having to be *likable* and *subordinate*, I had no more unconscious reason to be a pleaser. Tara stopped people-pleasing once she dropped *good/rescue*. Reba had the epiphany that she was OK no matter what and gave up her pleasing ways once she stopped being *obedient* and *pretending*. Once you overcome your words, your need to people-please will disappear.

I never actually thought much about being a people-pleaser. If I had to guess why, it's because I was too busy having to be *likable* all the time. Do I grasp the irony? You bet.

Inside our words we are never safe. How can we be? We're attached to an unwinnable outcome.

I realize saying sorry all the time is a byproduct of people-pleasing, but it is also a habit. One that can be trained out of us. It took a while to change that habit in myself because it was so deeply embedded that it came out unconsciously. Now, one will sneak out once in a blue moon, but for the most part, it's been replaced with my apologies: "I apologize, that's on me." "Excuse me, I didn't mean to _____." Or better yet, not saying anything at all if it's not warranted. If you need an easy cheat, you can try saying "bowling ball" to yourself. That might do it.

The Words Narcissists Love

> *"The narcissist is like a bucket with a hole in the*
> *bottom: No matter how much you put in, you can*
> *never fill it up. The phrase 'I never feel like I am*
> *enough' is the mantra of the person in a narcissistic*
> *relationship. That's because to your narcissistic*
> *partner, you are not. No one is. Nothing is."*
> **—Dr. Ramani Durvasula**[6]

Now, let's connect some dots regarding certain third and sixth words and their unconscious connection to narcissists. We're talking grandiose narcissist only right now. Some traits that come to mind: Entitled. Arrogant. Self-important. These are but a few that separate the narcissist from someone who is just an everyday jerk. Narcissists have no empathy—they have no capacity for it. They lack true emotion. They have zero tolerance for criticism or even perceived criticism. They are incapable of emotional intimacy. They don't feel a need to hide any of those traits for the simple reason that they don't care what you think. And they'll be charming as hell. At first. It'll be hard to resist having them in your life if you have a word that attracts one, because they love what you've got, and they'll charm your socks off to get you to stay their friend, spouse, sibling, caretaker, whatever.

The reason narcissists are so vibrant and
alive on the outside is because they're so
completely dead and empty on the inside.

One reoccurring theme that came across doing people's 7 Words is folks finding themselves in narcissistic relationships. Not once or twice, but over and over. There happen to be certain third and sixth words that draw narcissists in: third words like *good, nice, powerless, appease, obedient, easygoing, perfect* and *giving,* to name a few. Automatically, the persona of these words creates a vacuum which allows the narcissist quick and easy access to your power. Maybe it's not your third word, but rather a sixth word that allows them backstage access to your unseen susceptibilities. Words like *rescue, accommodate, stoic, give in, subordinate* (I can relate), *peacemaker* and *sabotage* allow more of a slow-burn or backdoor access to your energy. In other words, the narcissists don't need to force their will on some unsuspecting victim. Folks with these words are often ready and willing to simply hand their power over. And a narcissist will never, ever pass up free energy.

Now, none of these will guarantee a narcissist in your life in the future, but it may explain why you've had narcissistic attachments in your past. Or maybe even now.

Some I've spoken to find themselves falling for one narcissist after another, asking the same questions over and over: "I'm a giving, loving person. Why can't I ever get what I want and need back from others? Why am I the one who always gives in? Why do I have to make others happy? Why do my feelings always come second? How come I never feel heard?" Check your words. Narcissistic energy-sucking also occurs with our family and friends. Have a narcissistic sister/brother/mom/dad/child/friend/coworker who leaves you feeling drained, unappreciated, and shriveled up after even the smallest encounter? They will have no power over you if you learn to let go of your made-up story and not engage.

The grandiose or hedonistic narcissists feel a pedestal is where they belong, so hopefully the world will see their elevated status just as their pedestal-building partner does. The narcissist will stay in the relationship so long as they are revered, in the spotlight, and have all the perceived power. Ask Mia, a striking, accomplished professional with an advanced degree who was unknowingly married to a narcissist for decades. Her sixth word is *accommodate*. To that end, she went along with and did everything for her husband. "That's what we do in a relationship," she said proudly. We don't have the time or reams of paper to list everything she did for him and the marriage, but suffice to say, the pedestal was lofty. Lincoln Memorial–esque. Then one day, she asked something of him: to please get more involved helping their oldest daughter who was having ongoing medical issues. Mia herself was dealing with her own physical condition and needed him to pitch in. His involvement didn't happen. What did happen is that within three weeks, he found someone else and unceremoniously sat Mia down and told her all about this new woman as if it were Mia's doing. During the divorce process, she finally lashed out: "I never asked you for help with anything. Ever. I ask you to do one thing and you leave?" His response said it all: "If you had asked me to do something earlier, we would have never lasted this long." Harsh words. Yet one of the most honest responses a narcissist's mouth has ever uttered. Possibly ever. Mia is now conscious of her past actions and has gotten past beating herself up for all she blindly did in her marriage and how she thought she was *played*. She now realizes it was her own sleepwalking desire to be loved that never worked and she's let that go. Last time we spoke she was healthy and thriving. Content and in a new relationship. One without a pedestal.

Surprisingly, the person on a pedestal doesn't feel comfortable up there. They secretly want and need to be accountable. They end up literally and figuratively looking down on the person who put them up there. It's not only awkward but also causes undo stress on both involved. It doesn't work for either person, man or woman. (Or penguins named Penny and Tux.) It never does. Unless the person on a pedestal happens to be a narcissist.

Matthew from Chicago brought his girlfriend to his lake home in Michigan to propose. He wanted to make a big splash. Something memorable. A larger-than-life presentation. As they walked up the path to the picturesque cabin, there was something large hanging on the door. A giant ring he had chosen for the occasion—a full-size life-preserver ring with their names on it. The gesture was romantic. The result was as planned: she said yes, and they were soon married. The most interesting part of the story is not the oversized ring but the unconscious part it represented. You see, Matthew's sixth word is *rescue*. And his choosing a life preserver to symbolize his upcoming marriage was way beyond coincidence. More like a *parapraxis*—known colloquially as a "Freudian slip"—an inadvertent mistake that is thought to reveal a person's unconscious motives, wishes or attitudes.

Matt did unconsciously ***rescue*** her throughout their two-decades-long marriage. Along with everyone else in his life. He put his bride on a huge pedestal for their entire relationship, rescuing her from even the slightest perceived inconvenience. Maybe she was disoriented from being up so high, but one day after she found more energy from other sources, she shimmied down the pillar and said the marriage was over. He is now fully aware of her narcissistic ways which, in retrospect, are so clear and obvious.

He doesn't *rescue* any longer and that goes for his five siblings or any strangers he always had to "take care of." When I talk about rescuing, I don't mean saving someone from burning buildings, I'm referring to someone like Matt who put everyone else's needs above his. Even if they never asked for his help. Matt laughs about it all now that he's awake, aware and conscious. He's divorced and *never been happier*. His words, not mine. He even sent me this picture of the life preserver on the lake-house door he came across as a reminder of how far he'd come.

I don't profess to be an authority on narcissism or narcissists. But I have done extensive research along with decades of on-the-job training. What I do know for certain is that my words *likable* and *subordinate* kept me inside the gravitational pull of every narcissist I encountered. For me, no longer being beholden to my words meant the end of being under the spell of narcissists who are all about one thing only: getting energy from others to power themselves. I now keep my own energy, and any narcissist I come in contact with must go elsewhere for their energy fix. It's quite freeing.

As you become more aware of people's third words, some patterns emerge. One that comes to mind are words that you might see in a narcissist, words like *special, perform, noticed* or *important.* This does *not* mean that if you or someone you know has one of those words, they are a narcissist. They are just words you're more likely to see in a narcissist. Those words are plentiful in Hollywood and Washington, DC, but plenty of non-narcissists have them as well. The point here is our words play out differently for all of us. Even if we have the same words.

We read how Kevin's third word *special* was something that drove him to seek validation by being that person people rely on to be there for them. He felt special when someone, anyone, thought or felt well of him. His feeling *special* played out on an intimate, one-on-one basis. Centered entirely on the feeling of being *special.* But a woman I know well named Monica* also has the third word *special.* Her word is completely driven by the appearance or perception of

---

* Full disclosure: Of all the people and stories I have used for this book not directly involving me, Monica is the only person I have not interviewed regarding Their 7 Words. I have known Monica for over three decades and know as much about her as anyone. My pronouncement of her third word SPECIAL comes from decades of up-close, personal observations and interactions with her in conjunction with my knowledge and understanding of the 7 Words. I have done the 7 Words of a few vulnerable narcissists but haven't come across a grandiose narcissist willing to do their words as far as I can tell. My guess is that vulnerable narcissists will do Their 7 Words because they don't want to be left out. Grandiose narcissists won't do Their 7 Words for fear of being found out. I may someday be proven wrong. But not so far.

being unique, extraordinary and, dare I say, superior. I have heard Monica replay the following story countless times. As she tells it, her family comes from Prussian royalty! Prussia was once the dominant state of Germany and as the story goes, her relatives were members of the exiled royal family after the Nazi government took over their country. They escaped in the dark of night with only a few suitcases and the Prussian crown jewels. The story concludes with her royal family using the crown jewels to trade for food and shelter and to fund their journey to safety where they survived WWII.

The "stories" people tell and repeat are intrinsically linked to their 7 Word Story, albeit unconsciously. Let's take Monica, for instance. Her third word *special* is her persona. The person telling this story wants to be *special*. Correction—needs to be *special*. And the story is told to make that person seem just that. If Monica's third word were, let's say, *giving* or *good*, that story would be useless in reinforcing that narrative. The desired outcome of what that story is telling her about who she is and who she needs to be to get love is rather obvious: she must find ways, or people, that validate her need to be special.

Before uncovering the 7 Words, I viewed Monica's Prussian royalty story as cute and harmless. A bit braggadocio but innocent enough. Now, I see it for what it really is—an attempt to reinforce the perception that the person telling it is nothing short of *special*. Monica also attempts to show the world she's *special* by needing to be the smartest person in a room. When she can't be the smartest, she must be special by befriending or being acknowledged by the smartest person. Or, as I have witnessed numerous times, bond with or latch onto the most powerful, popular or attractive person in the room. Male or female. She once sat next to a celebrity at a dinner and later bragged how she drank from this special person's water glass, making Monica special by association.

Kevin and Monica, one third word, *special*. Two different manifestations.

Spotting narcissists, whether you know their third/sixth word or not, is a tricky challenge. If you're in the entertainment industry or politics, it would be easier to pick out a non-narcissist. Outside of Wilshire Boulevard and the Capital Beltway, it's a bit more difficult. They look very much like everyone else, but they are run by their third and sixth words just the way we are. The only difference is that their words are turbocharged by their narcissistic tendencies.

With that in mind, I put my advertising background to good use and created my own line of NarcissistBumperStickers™ for fun . . . and to remind myself and others not to give our power away to anyone. Especially a narcissist. Here are a few:

> Narcissists suck . . . the life out of you.

> Narcissists love a give-and-take relationship.
> You give, they take.

> Apathy: kryptonite to the narcissist.

> Narcissists are like stray cats.
> If you stop feeding them (your energy)
> they will go somewhere else.

> Your relationship with a
> narcissist is like a two-person cult.
> Guess who's the follower and who's the leader.

When we put someone on a
pedestal, we take them off the hook.

Through the connecting of dots and my own experience and foibles, I know firsthand the monument game is a setup for failure and will help sabotage the relationship. The person is perched on the platform and suddenly has no accountability whatsoever. The one who placed the person up there has abdicated power, authority, and any chance of a functional relationship. We can't say that the balance of power is out of whack because there is no balance whatsoever. Speaking of lack of balance, being in a relationship with a narcissist is the epitome of such a tilting of the scales. Maybe you've been in a relationship or two or five with a narcissist. Reba was. Tara, Mia, and Vin were too. Add Matt from Chicago to the list. All have broken that unconscious need to please or be with a narcissist. They're now very aware of what that looks like, or more importantly, what that is. The word is "dysfunctional." No other way to put it. Any relationship with a narcissist is a dysfunctional one by default. The first obvious reason being that you work for them. And there is a very simple principle the narcissist relationship runs on. They need constant energy, and you will give them all they need. Simple.

Let's put it into a word we've been using throughout this entire book: attention. Narcissists can't live without it. I'm going to dispel the myth that narcissists think they are better, smarter, prettier, or more deserving than the rest of us. Not true. Narcissists actually have lower self-esteem and are more insecure than the rest of us. And the more insecure they are, the more control they need to exert. Which is why narcissists need endless reassurance and praise. That comes in the form of energy. They need it; and they will find it most of the time from, you guessed it, people-pleasers. Narcissists will put out maybe 5 percent of their energy to get back 95 percent from others. They will often find people who require even less output than 5 percent. As we spoke of earlier, certain third and sixth words are magnets for narcissists. And if you are one of those people, you hand most of your energy over to your narcissist, and whatever energy you may have left you use to try to get them to pay attention to you for a change. It won't happen. For the simple reason that they are in an all-out covert competition with you every single day. But you're unaware of it. You won't be getting their emotions or their empathy either. They're incapable of both. Simply put, narcissistic relationships, even ones with siblings or parents, are completely one-sided. There is only one surefire way to keep your energy and sanity: don't engage. If you don't give them your energy, they will go somewhere else, and find a people-pleaser that will.

Reverse the Cycle

Regarding the story you now can't unknow, your newfound knowledge will be bumping into that "dysfunctional orbit" you were unconsciously in. At some point you will run through the cycle of Your 7 Words just as you have for years, maybe decades, and you'll have a realization: *I just did it again. I had to be [my third/ persona word] and I became [my sixth word] when things inevitably went sideways.* Now **repeat** has you back to **invisible**. You will realize what just happened because you're aware of the story and now "know your cycle." You'll probably beat yourself up a bit, then soldier on. It may happen again a time or two or four and you'll get annoyed and tell yourself, *I did it again. I went all the way around and got to **rescue, pull away, sabotage, run, analyze, stoic** . . .* whatever your sixth word is.

You'll find yourself inside your third word and realize you're on a collision course with your fourth, fifth, sixth and seventh and it will feel different this time. You'll unexpectedly catch yourself. The best way to explain it was actually feeling my third word trying to click in and attempting to take over.

One day there came a moment that flipped the script—a turning point in my development. The uncovering of my words happened a few months prior, and I was meeting a woman for a first date. She was a former professional ballerina turned ballet teacher (feel free to smirk, I am). We talked, laughed, and after a few glasses of wine, walked to a club nearby. We were dancing and having a nice time tearing up the parquet floor (my interpretation) when the song changed to something slower. She walked to our table, quickly finished her cocktail, zigzagged across the dance floor and straight out the front door. Momentarily confused, I then made my way through the crowd and out to the packed sidewalk, catching up to her at the valet stand around the corner. She turned and, in a faux affected voice directed more toward the valet, said, "Are you stalking me?" Without missing a beat, I said to the valet, "We've been on a date for the past two hours; she walked off the dance floor, finished her drink and left without saying a word." Turning to her, I calmly, with direct eye contact, said, "You are without a doubt the rudest person I've ever met," and I walked away. Plopping down on a bench around the block, I felt my heart pounding. Not a fight-or-flight thumping; this was excitement. Exhilaration. Even giving myself a goofy high five for calmly confronting someone directly and taking care of me. Maybe I wasn't Baryshnikov in her mind, but what was more important was that I didn't have to be *likable* or *subordinate* in mine. Not time to retire the sleepwalking slippers yet, but it was a monster of a breakthrough moment.

Others who have done their words and broken free of them have shared stories of how they felt their words creeping up and either caught themselves right after they slipped into their word or eventually understood the situation and felt themselves pull out of it and literally break their word cycle. I not only want this for you, but I also know that if you do the work that follows, you will be there as well. The work that follows for you is to eliminate your overthinking about all this and trust the process. Trust that your unconscious self has delivered those words to you because it knows you best. Quiet your mind in whatever way works for you. Like I suggested, use eye shades and noise-cancelling headphones and set a timer for five minutes at first. Just own your words. Your emotions. You've done an incredible job of working your way through all this and now you've set yourself up to shed your sabotaging ways.

What happened with me in my ballerina-date story is that was the first time I didn't unconsciously slip into my 7 Word Story. I was completely aware in the moment and wasn't seeing the world through my *likable* mask. My reaction was completely honest, organic and one hundred percent in the moment.

When we hear about mindfulness and awareness, this is exactly what we're speaking of. Seeing everything around us in real time. Looking back, I knew I was aware of the moment because I could see the ballerina was projecting to the valet and pretending to be speaking to me. My response was to the valet first, then to her. Before my words, I would have had to be unconsciously *likable*. Being conscious and aware gave me the freedom and power to have these interactions calmly, without voices raised or a fight-or-flight response. In complete control. That's the power of understanding and accepting our words. It took me a few times of catching myself pass *likable* and pull up before *subordinate*. Eventually, the light turns on and we see the moments in HD for the first time. Trust me, you'll be as excited the first time it happens to you as I was. I can't wait to hear your success story personally.

14

Keys to Self-Acceptance, Not Self-Love

At our core, what we want and need is to be accepted, appreciated and loved for who we are. And safely be us doing it. Up until a few years ago—or, BW (before words)—I not only didn't feel any of those things but I had no idea who I truly was. As I said earlier, my outward facade was easygoing, happy-go-lucky, unbothered Jerry who was likable to one and all. That was all there to cover up the fear that someone would find out the truth—that I was just a scared little kid on a park bench.

Apparently, I'm not the only one. While reading Rob Lowe's autobiography, I stumbled upon this line: "If you *really* knew me, you wouldn't like me nearly as much."[1] After reading that line, I yelled, "Holy crap! Rob Lowe too?" That can't be. Look at his life. His career. Look at HIM! Then there was me pretending daily that everything was OK but feeling inside that it was a lie. Covering up my missing puzzle pieces and judging my insides by other people's outsides. Maybe it sounds incredibly self-absorbed on my part, thinking I was the only person who didn't feel real or good about myself, the only person who doubted my worth and put myself down. Not a movie star. Not someone who seemingly has it all. Not Rob *freakin'* Lowe! (Going back to what I said earlier about the abundance of narcissists in Hollywood, Rob Lowe is not one of them. No narcissist would ever admit what he did in his book. Even though they all deep down believe it.)

The Quest for Self-esteem

Throughout my life there always existed a silent undercurrent of low self-esteem. As an experiment, I sat down and Googled "How to build self-esteem." Try it if you like, but I can save you some time by showing many of the results. Quite a few—nearly all of them in fact—will not only seem familiar but you've either heard them before, or have a fridge magnet, pillow, mug, journal cover, or cell phone case with one or more of these sayings on it; you might've even written them down on an inspiration board somewhere. Surely you have a few of them highlighted in yellow in numerous books on your bookshelf:

Be nice to yourself. Eliminate self-criticism. Challenge your limiting beliefs. Stop worrying what others think. Let negative people go. Face your fears. Think positive. Forgive yourself. Encourage yourself. Stop sabotaging yourself. Fake it till you make it. Talk nicely to yourself. Say goodbye to perfection. Love yourself. Keep smiling no matter what. Shape your own self-image. Change your story.

Many if not most of these affirmations are words we've heard hundreds of times. There's nothing wrong with any of these thoughts. They're cute, playful, seemingly helpful—not to mention, popular. What they aren't is successful at creating long-term fulfillment. The reason: <u>WE DON'T BELIEVE THEM!</u> We're wired to *not* believe them. We don't throw away a lifetime of self-doubt, sabotaging behaviors, or unhealthy thinking just because some article tells us to. Another attempt at left-brain logic attempting to solve our right-brain emotional issue.

Let's go back to the last item on our how-to-build-self-esteem list: *Change your story.* Awesome suggestion. The big question is *how?*

How do I "change my story" or do *any* of those things on the list for that matter? First, we need to find out <u>WHAT OUR STORY IS!</u> Not to state the obvious, but that's exactly what we just did by uncovering Your 7 Word Story. The one that's had you handcuffed since preschool. Now, that emotional story we created can be seen for what it actually is: a roadblock to our true selves and our self-esteem. That's because self-esteem is also an emotional issue inherently tied to our made-up story. By taking your story into your own hands, self-esteem comes along for the ride.

Once we become mindful of our thoughts, feelings, and especially our behaviors, we can disconnect from the autopilot we've been running on and become conscious and operate from a place of awareness. This applies to you, me, and even someone as cool as Mr. Rob Lowe. No, self-awareness is not a guarantee of contentment or happiness. But without it, understanding what's not working in our lives is virtually impossible.

Some Thoughts on that Four-Letter Word . . . Self-Love.

That's two four-letter words if you're counting at home. Mathematics aside, the notion known as "self-love"—the holy grail of perpetual happiness—is constantly being preached at every turn. But just as our 7 Word Story is a repeated failure, so is our endless search for self-love. But the word "love" itself is a Pandora's box. Better yet, a tinderbox packed with hopes, trappings, and unreachable (here comes another reoccurring word) . . . expectations. It means something different to all of us. If you asked a thousand people what their definition of "love" is, you'll most likely get one thousand and two different answers.

I polled a number of people and asked them to respond to a simple question: "What does the word 'love' mean to you?" Here are some of their exact, unedited responses.

- *It makes you feel good on the inside.*
- *It's stronger than an emotion and something you can actually feel.*
- *There's an unconscious smile when you see that person.*
- *A feeling—something you just can't explain; you just know that it's special.*
- *You are committed to a person completely and they are committed to you.*
- *An intangible connection that's deeply rooted in spirit.*
- *You trust each other with your souls.*

Apparently, the word love has more overstuffed baggage than JFK Airport during Thanksgiving week. As we speak, someone is writing a song, a screenplay, a poem, or a social media post about the L word. There are more "love songs" than any other type. Followed closely, of course, by heartbreak ballads.

As we have seen, there are as many definitions of love as there are people hopelessly searching high and low for it. Even if we miraculously find our perfect love, as yours truly once believed he had, we might not fit the other person's definition of what love is to them. Sure, we may ask our lover what their "love language" is. Now we know theirs is affirmation or quality time, great! But no one asks the other person what their definition of love is.

But here's the point: The word "love" and all the feelings that go along with it are so perplexing, mystifying, and tenuous, the fact that we somehow believe we can make it relevant to us by simply inserting the word "self" in front of it is nonsensical. Yet, self-love has become a magic pill, the cure-all for all our woes across the entire fix-it, self-help spectrum. We hear we can't love others until we love ourselves. Again, what is *love*? If we can accept ourselves for who we are then, and only then, do we have any shot at accepting someone else for who *they* are? Turns out, our quest for self-love, our 7 Word Story, and the unconscious bowling ball, are all setups for failure.

I want to go on record that I am not anti-love at all, but rather an optimistic, eternal, hopeful romantic and a lover of love and all that goes with it. I have just learned that now that I accept myself for who I am, I'm able to accept everyone in my life for who they are. Especially the person I am in love with. For me, acceptance is love without the guessing and expectations.

If we take out the word *love* from "self-love" and add the word "acceptance," it changes the entire paradigm. The thing about acceptance is that we either accept something or we don't. If we accept something, we acknowledge or receive it as it is with no judgment. Let's be honest, acceptance is more elusive than love. The thought of love sounds loftier and more magical. But as we have seen from our words, magical is not very grounded. Acceptance is nothing but grounded.

If we say, "Honey, I accept you for who you are, but . . . ," the acceptance is automatically conditional—therefore, not acceptance at all. Not unlike the unconscious conditional attention which drove us to our third word all those many years ago. That attention and "love" we were attached to the outcome of was conditional. True acceptance, on the other hand, has no conditions attached.

This distinction finally allowed me to unconditionally accept myself for who I am. Accept my sleepwalking for what it was. Accept little jerry, Big Jerry, I-have-to-be-*likable* Jerry, I-became-*subordinate* Jerry, petrified-of-confrontation Jerry. Accept them, yes, but I don't, nor will I ever, love that I have to be *likable* and *subordinate* Jerry. I won't love fearful, gave-his-ex-wife-the-finger-behind-her-back-hundreds-of-times-because-he-was-living-in-fear Jerry. But accepting those Jerrys for who they were at the time and accepting My 7 Words as something that unconsciously ran me, that changed the game. Now, I've learned to unconditionally accept everything I have done in my life without judgment, unconditionally accept everything I *haven't* done in my life without judgment, unconditionally accept everyone I know and meet for who they are without judgment. I do my best to deal with what shows up in front of me at the moment and move on.

This is a reminder I created that helped me and others not only understand the power of acceptance but literally accept it into our daily lives.

The Contentment through Acceptance Pyramid

Peace
Freedom
Contentment

7. I live my life as best I can in unconditional acceptance...

6. I unconditionally accept everyone in the world for who they are without judgement...

5. I unconditionally accept everyone I know and everyone I meet for who they are without judgement...

4. I unconditionally accept everything I "percieve" people haven't done for me without judgement...

3. I unconditionally accept everything I "percieve" people have done to me without judgement

2. I unconditionally accept everything I haven't done in my life without judgement...

1. I unconditionally accept everything I have done in my life so far without judgement...

Exit the endless circle of Your 7 Words and ascend to the top of the safety, freedom, and contentment pyramid.

Only after accepting what you did or who you were in the past can you accept yourself for who you are now. If you notice one thing about all of these statements, it should be that they say unconditionally "accept"... there is nothing that mentions you have to *like* any of those things, people, or events. Accepting and liking what you accept are two different things. The reason I can accept all of them is because I understand I can't change them. If you have any issues letting go of any of the above (I did at first), just ask yourself, "Would I do it again?" If the answer is no, accept it and *let go*!

Acceptance always comes before
freedom in the dictionary. And in life.

When I accept all I've done or haven't done in my past, there's a sense of letting go, a sovereignty and autonomy I had no idea was possible. When we unconditionally accept ourselves, we break free of the ego and find freedom and safety in who we are. That allows us to work exclusively from our own personal power base with no need to look elsewhere.

While we're on the topic of self-love and self-acceptance, this seems like the perfect opportunity to discuss the ever-elusive concept of self-esteem, which is possibly as overanalyzed, over-probed and misconstrued as either of the other two. My self-esteem, or lack thereof, was mentioned quite often throughout this book. It not only eluded me but seemed completely beyond my comprehension. But once I discovered my words and fully embraced uncondoned acceptance, the fears I carried with me my entire life slid away. The fear was replaced with safety. Which led me to not only discover my self-esteem but a clear and simple definition of it. To me, self-esteem is *knowing no matter what happens I will be OK*. It's that simple. Yes, it does take some work to get to simplicity, but once you get there, the hardest thing is trying to stop smiling.

We have been exploring acceptance and how it relates to contentment and freedom. We can't talk enough about those words because they are the key to your peaceful, nonjudgmental future. Getting us to a place of acceptance and letting go of our expectations and judgments is what mindfulness is all about.

Simply put: mindfulness isn't about constantly learning new stuff, but about unlearning our old stuff.

If overthinking solved all of our problems, you, me and most of us would be without a care in the world by now.

The following poem was inspired by my own 7 Word discovery and the surprising realization that I wasn't the only person who felt "broken" out there.

EVERYBODY'S BROKEN
by Jerry Giordano

Everybody's broken, the big and the small,
Yup, we're all quite broken, welcome one and all.

Maybe you weren't smart enough, neat enough, or perfect in every way,
Afraid they'd punish you, leave you—or the worst: ignore what you say.
Self-help preaches we're wonderful, amazing, and complete without a doubt,
It's a momentary self-esteem sugar rush we all too soon find out.

Everybody's broken, we don't come that way,
Inside it grows and emerges one day.
We're all held together with false bravado and boast,
Not so deep down we realize we're no better than most.
Nobody gets a pass—janitor, politician, or BIG movie star,
We all see it in our reflections, no need to look very far.
Incredible job, hot car or body, wow, look what they've got,
Everybody's broken, even if appearances scream they're not.

We all have our secret not good enough that no one knows,
The more we try to cover or control it the more it grows.

We didn't feel unconditional love we wanted from Mother,
Or felt as smart, talented, or (fill in the blank) as sister or brother.

We do the dog dance and pony show just to get by,
People usually buy it, but we know it's really a lie.
Our attempts to be perfect, good, helpful, likable, nice, or sweet,
Mask the someone deep inside we're afraid others might meet.

We're all broken about something that no one else knows,
When the lights go out and it's just us, our not good enough glows.
If we ever told others what our not good enough might be,
Most would laugh, think us crazy, it's something only we see.

We judge our insides by other's outsides, that's what we do,
Only way to be unbroken is to look at ourselves anew.
See our not good enough as that untrue story a three-year-old created,
A blanket of self-protection with no power, it's time to be liberated.

To all the people like me who believed they were broken and not good
enough, I have some important news to share:
The good news: We're not better than anyone else.
The great news: Nobody else is better than us.

My Tips for Self-Acceptance

Lose the self. No, not "Lose Yourself," as in the Eminem anthem, but lose the word "self" from self-acceptance. What you have then is simply acceptance. By taking the self out of the equation, we are opening up to the power of the universal *higher* power. Then we can focus on the operative word: acceptance. When we accept things in our past and present that we cannot change, we are freeing ourselves. When we accept the people in our lives for who they are without judgment, we free ourselves. When we accept people we don't know, and especially the ones we disagree with, without judgment, we free ourselves. Again, I can't stress this point enough: *You do not have to like anyone or anything to accept them.*

Next time you're on social media, reading, watching or listening to the news (or the n'EW's as I prefer to call it), or involved in a discussion about politics or anything that invokes a point of view that you may disagree with, accept what they're saying for what it is—an opinion—and let it go. That goes for our own beliefs as well. We should treat our opinions like sex. Unless someone asks us to join in, we should keep it to ourselves.

And if you can't let any of this go, shut it down. None of what we just mentioned will give you anything other than a predetermined emotional tirade and pull you directly out of acceptance (function) and directly into judgment (dysfunction). Honestly, it can't be any simpler.

Early on in this book we shared some illuminating words from Carl Jung. It seems only fitting that we start winding down with his unmatched wisdom as well.

Who looks outside dreams. Who looks inside awakes.[2]

The only thing I care to add to that is, "It's a great day to be AWAKE!"

Finally, Freedom from Fear

> *To little jerry, wherever you are, thank you.*
> *I LOVE YOU MORE . . .*

I have shared some personal moments of my life with you. In some ways my hardest and most difficult. Yet, I have no desire to compare my experiences to yours or anyone else's. We all have overcome obstacles, and many have had it much worse with so much more heartache than me. But my journey and my rock bottom were real. My job isn't to give my voyage any more or less importance than yours or anyone else's, but to share the understanding and self-discovery that changed my world. And I know firsthand it has done the same for many who have uncovered their words as well.

In many ways I'm grateful for my crash and descent into that foreboding abyss back in 2017. It's what helped transform my sleepwalking into waking. To that end, I've learned to unconditionally accept my ex-wife and ex-fiancée for who they are without malice, acrimony or blame. They too were sleepwalking and most likely still are. But that's out of my control. What is important is that I've learned to take 50 percent responsibility for the breakdown and failure of those and all the other relationships in my life. Not 51 percent or 49 percent. Just my sleepwalking half, which was entirely driven by my unconscious *invisible*, *unloved*, *likable*, *control*, *frustration*, *subordinate* and *repeat* that ran me and sabotaged my relationships with others and myself. Being accountable for my half alone and letting go of their half has brought me unimaginable peace, along with accepting them for who they are. Because they have no idea any of this is occurring, they most likely won't be taking their half of responsibility for their roles in our relationships just like most, if not all, of your unknowing former partners won't. But it's not about them, it's about us releasing our part. Taking accountability for our half and nothing and more nothing less, that will allow you to release and finally let go of the angst, the sorrow, pain, disappointment, and anger you're holding onto. In other words, accept them for who they are and move on.

Notice that nowhere did I say you have to like or love them. Accepting frees us from all those other entanglements. We can accept every single person in our life—and the world—without having any obligation to like them. Inside that nuance is where the freeing magic lies.

Conscious awareness has brought me self-honest behavior I never thought possible. That has gifted me acceptance and contentment which, in turn, has given rise to freedom. The foundation of acceptance became the alchemy that transformed me from judgmental pawn to the mountaintop of contentment and freedom. My 7 Words are still with me, but they don't run my life any longer. That has given me peace, understanding, and possibly the greatest gift of all—meaning in my life. It has since propelled me to a place of self-actualization symbolized by what I like to call F^3. My new consciousness equation. F^3 = Freedom from Fear.

Freedom to do and to be better.

Happiness, the Tooth Fairy and Finding a Birkin Bag at a Thrift Store. Urban Myths One and All.

The title of this book is not *Your 7 Words to Happiness*. It's *to a Happier You*—as in being better off than you were before reading this.

How ironic that we are forever chasing lasting happiness in a world of endless change.

The lure of happiness sells cars, vacations, jewelry, beer, mortgages and diapers. Snoopy cartoonist Charles Schulz gave us the line, "Happiness is a warm puppy." Everywhere we look, we're being sold happiness and for good reason; most of us are obsessed with finding it. That only causes happiness to become the split second that occurs before we start looking for more happiness. As I have learned the hard way, happiness is not an outcome. Not something you can touch, grab, or possess. Until I discovered meditation and uncovered my unconscious sabotaging story half a year later, I chased happiness daily like Wile E. Coyote raced after the Road Runner, often with similar results. Attached to the outcome of being "happy" for most of my life, I didn't know what I didn't know. The truth was, like the simplicity of the ruby slippers in the *Wizard of Oz*, Dorothy, you, and I *always had the power.* Not for the esoteric happiness, but what the ancient Greeks called *epimeleia heautou,* or "care of the self"— actions exercised on the self by the self, actions by which one takes responsibility for oneself, and by which one changes, purifies, and transforms oneself.

This is all done consciously. "Until you make the unconscious conscious, it will direct your life and you will call it fate." When I finally accepted myself for being unconscious, I was able to accept my pre-discovery sleepwalking self and my self-sabotaging ways. Acceptance of myself, then of others, led directly to inner peace. That led to safety, knowing that no matter what happened, I was going to be OK. Which brought me to contentment with how I was and am right now, free of inner conflicts and ultimately unattached to outcome. Aka, free.

The Buddha's wisdom that "attachment is the root of suffering" is simple and significant. I finally realized my attachment to my perpetual search for happiness brought me only suffering. And more unhappiness. When I first began my meditation practice in October 2016, I inadvertently created a mantra. I was just trying to give myself something to concentrate on to avoid distractions. Inhaling, I thought of the word *let,* and exhaling, the word *go* appeared. It worked. And to this day, if I find my mind wandering in meditation, I repeat *LET . . . GO, LET . . . GO* with rhythmic breaths.

I didn't realize it at the time, but that was the beginning of me finally being able to *let go* of a lot of things that held me back all my life. I let go of my feelings of not being good enough. I let go of my worry about the past and anxiety about the future. I let go of my PPP (persistent people-pleasing). And I let go of *invisible → unloved → likable → control → frustration → subordinate → repeat.*

What I replaced all those with was acceptance, safety, inner peace, contentment, and freedom.

I used to buy into the myth that happiness was a skill. I couldn't have been more off. Happiness is the trap. Letting go is the skill—and the answer.

I can't wait to hear about how you're *letting go of your old story so you can start your new life.*

Then we can teach everyone we love how to be functional in a dysfunctional world.

(I think I may have the next book title. That brings me ~~happiness~~ contentment.)

Conclusion

Throughout history, the mythological story of Sisyphus has been analyzed, decoded, and interpreted. The origin of this story comes from the mythological king Sisyphus who was punished for tricking the gods. Hades—king of the underworld—condemned Sisyphus to roll a boulder up a steep hill only to have it roll back down when he neared the top. He then had to repeat the action over and over. For eternity.

The philologist Friedrich Gottlieb Welcker believed that Sisyphus symbolizes man's struggle for knowledge. Franz Kafka was intrigued by the absurdity of the story. French philosopher and Nobel Prize winner Albert Camus probed the topic deeply when he wrote the essay *The Myth of Sisyphus*. In an appendix to that essay titled "Hope and the Absurd in the Works of Franz Kafka," Camus took a more hopeful path when he wrote, "Within the limits of the human condition, what greater hope than the hope that allows an escape from that condition?"[3]

I found the appendix compelling. Not only *hope* to escape from our "condition," but hope to overcome its hold on us. I am hoping that you have not only uncovered Your 7 Words, but put that learning toward creating a happier you.

With all my numerous successes and many more failures, it can be said without any doubt whatsoever that I'm the most content, satisfied, and happiest I've ever been in my adult life. All this comes as a byproduct of jettisoning my old sabotaging story and embracing my new conscious awareness.

It's been said by others far smarter than me that the greatest achievement for any of us is to find meaning in our time here on earth and become who we're truly meant to be. In the meditation scene from City Slickers, the character had to figure out what his "one thing" was. I found mine, and I knew if I could somehow gently shake others from sleepwalking through life and help turn their unconscious ways into conscious actions, I had no other alternative but to attempt to do so. Not merely a book for me, in my mind *Your 7 Words to a Happier You* is my reason for being here. To share the discovery that changed my everything and "pay it forward" to others like you.

For what it's worth, writing a book wasn't something that was planned. But then again, neither was having multiple panic attacks, being stunned, staggered, shattered, and depressed either. Life happens. So do opportunities. And if we work hard, get lucky, and connect some dots, solutions start to appear. All those experiences led to this book.

Now you know that what you thought you had to be—your third-word persona—is really a no-win situation you don't even have to play. That means there are no boulders nearby ready to roll over you. Unlike Sisyphus, you can pull yourself out of the game—just as I did. You now have the tools and the information you need to connect the dots to your own freedom. Armed with the right-brain solution of *why* you sabotaged your relationships and yourself all those years, you are well on your path to acceptance, mindfulness, and freedom.

And by the way, sitting by a still boulder is a nice place to find peace.

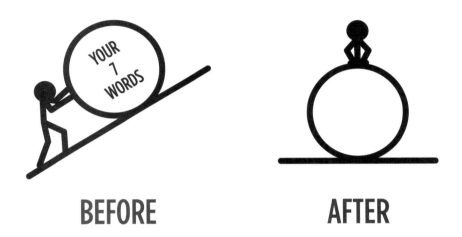

BEFORE   **AFTER**

Acknowledgments

To my three beautiful kiddos, Harper, Zane, and Hugo. I unconditionally accept and love you *meeces to pieces*. To my ceaseless confidant Peyton "Doc" Wimmer, who taught me more about the human psyche than any library ever could, and whose friendship, care, and pragmatism was an unwavering tether through my hard place and rock bottom. To Jimmy "Mel" Palumbo—my brother from the same grandmother—who has never not been there for me. I would trust him with my life—and have. Thank you, Mel, for never judging my babblings, no matter how incoherent. To Reverend Lee at the Agape Spiritual Center in Frisco, Texas, for introducing me to unconditional acceptance and for your spiritual nourishment during my murkiest days. To my enlightenment counselor, Bernadette Smith—grace personified. Your spiritual interpretations and sweet guiding voice were immeasurable. You listened to my boohoo baboonery and still you guided me with compassion, wisdom, and light. To another beautiful soul and confidante, Linda Beugg, for schooling me on the finding and trusting of my spiritual voice. Even though you're a Red Sox fan, you're beyond amazing! To design goddess and dear friend, Tracey Locke, for her design help with this and many other projects. To *il mio migliore amico* (my best friend)

215

and consiglieri Rob Soluri. Thanks for your unending loyalty and trust. Your friendship means the world to me, my brotha'.

To my daydream believer and unceasing advocate, Tamie. Your generosity, respect and understanding knows no bounds. Thank you for all you have done to support this project and help make this 7 Words process and book progress, blossom, and thrive.

A special thanks to reporter/author Dan Harris and his book *10% Happier*. After attempting to meditate for twenty-plus years, it was Dan's book that finally closed my eyes and untied my mind to meditation just three months before my descent into my darkest days. It not only helped me survive those overwhelming crossroads, but to ultimately accept them. Thank you, Dan, for having a panic attack on live television in front of five million viewers, bringing you to meditation and to ultimately write your life-altering book. Both of which moved me to do the same. I'm forever in your debt and have gifted *10% Happier* to many folks and will continue to do so.

Throughout this intense project, there were surprisingly few moments of faltering conviction. My meditation practice along with my gut held the line for all four quarters. "This will make a difference in people's lives" was the rebel yell from most interviewees. The oldest and possibly the most mind-blowing of which was Dr. W. Norman, MD, age 94, who, after getting to and discussing his 7 Words, ended our conversation with, "Your book is going to be amazing. There isn't a book on this subject." That, of course, was satisfying to hear from a world-renowned MD who studied at the Royal College of Surgery in London and eventually became one of the founders of one of the country's premier medical schools.

To my gifted partners at Brown Books Publishing Group. My first salute must go to my content editor, Sterling Hooker, who tamed my overenthusiasm and kept me focused throughout. Her unflappable guidance was surpassed only by her thoughtful and calming demeanor. Sterling is the gold standard in editing. To Brittany Griffiths, my project manager, who kept the train not only on schedule but literally on the tracks. A thankless job that deserves endless thanks. To Amy Goppert, my publicity manager, who sees chess moves far into the future. Thank you for your inventiveness and passion. Cheers to designer Danny Whitworth. I may have uncovered the 7 Words, but he put an inspirational cover over them. To my line editor, Ben Davidoff, who, like a world-class surgeon, used his skills, keen eye and metaphorical scalpel to carve, trim and remove even the tiniest imperfections. Much appreciated. And lastly, to the *Capo di tutti capi*, Milli Brown, whose vision and inspiration are felt in every aspect of the astonishing company she built. The Godmother's love of words and books is obvious in everything she does, and her stylish elegance fills every room she enters. Milli and I bonded over our love of communication, and our obsession with each other's shoes. My sole mate. Thank you, Milli, for everything you bring to your staff, your authors, and the world at large. My passion project became everyone's at Brown Books, and for that I will be eternally grateful.

Notes

Chapter 1

1. Victor Frankl, *Man's Search for Meaning* (Boston: Beacon Press, 2006).

Chapter 3

1. Kendra Cherry, "The Unconscious Mind, Preconscious Mind and Conscious Mind," *Verywell Mind*, February 27, 2023, https://www.verywellmind.com/the-conscious-and-unconscious-mind-2795946.

2. *Alchemical Studies (Collected Works of C. G. Jung Vol. 13)*, ed. Sir Herbert Read et al., trans. Gerhard Adler, Bollingen Series XX (New York: Princeton University Press, 1983), 266.

Chapter 4

1. Paul C. Hollinger, "The Origins of Our Emotional Life: Our Earliest Feelings," *Psychology Today*, July 1, 2016, author referencing Janet Browne's *Charles Darwin: A Biography, Vol. 2: The Power of Place* (Knopf, 2002), https://www.psychology today.com/us/blog/great-kids-great-parents/201607/the-origins-our-emotional-life-our-earliest-feelings.

3. Peter R. Huttenlocher, *Neural Plasticity: The Effects of Environment on the Development of the Cerebral Cortex (Perspectives in Cognitive Neuroscience)* (Harvard Press, 2002).

4. Australian Children's Education & Care Quality Authority, "Brain Development in Children" entry, StartingBlocks.gov, last updated January 23, 2024, https://startingblocks.gov.au/resources/parenting-and-home/your-childs-development/brain-development-in-children.

5. Barbara Dautrich, "How is magical thinking a normal and protective part of early child development?", Quora forum, 2020, https://www.quora.com/How-is-magical-thinking-a-normal-and-protective-part-of-early-child-development/answer/Barbara-Dautrich.

6. "Foundation: Cause-and-Effect," Specialized Programs page, California Department of Education, last modified January 10, 2024, https://www.cde.ca.gov/sp/cd/re/itf09cogdevfdcae.asp.

7. John Stuart Mill, *Utilitarianism*, Project Gutenberg, February 1, 2004, https://www.gutenberg.org/cache/epub/11224/pg11224-images.html.

8. Eve R. Colson and Paul H. Dworkin, "Toddler Development," *Pediatrics in Review*, vol. 18, no. 8 (August 1997): 259, https://depts.washington.edu/dbpeds/ToddlerDvt.pdf.

9. Eve R. Colson and Paul H. Dworkin, "Toddler Development."

Chapter 5

1. George Beahm, ed., *I, Steve: Steve Jobs in His Own Words*, (Chicago: Agate, 2011).

2. *The Collected Works of C. G. Jung (Complete Digital Edition)*, ed. Gerhard Adler and trans. R. F. C. Hull, vol. 8, Bollingen Series XX (New York: Princeton University Press), 483, https://wellcord.org/wp-content/plugins/pdfjs-viewer-shortcode/pdfjs/web/viewer.php?file=https://wellcord.org/

wp-content/uploads/2021/10/8-CG-JUNG-Collected
-Works-of-CG-Jung-Volume-8_-Structure-Dynamics-of-
the-Psyche-2.pdf&attachment_id=&dButton=true&
pButton=true&oButton=false&s Button=true.

10. *The Collected Works of C. G. Jung (Complete Digital Edition)*,
ed. Adler et al, trans. R. F. C. Hull, vol. 17, Bollingen Series
XX (New York, N.Y.: Princeton University Press), 179,
https://jungiancenter.org/wp-content/uploads/2023/09/
vol-17-the-development-of-personality.pdf.

11. Rick Lyman, "Marlon Brando, Oscar-Winning Actor,
Is Dead at 80," *New York Times*, July 2, 2004, https://
www.nytimes.com/2004/07/02/movies/marlon-brando-
oscarwinning-actor-is-dead-at-80.html.

Chapter 11

1. Rachel Allyn, "The Important Difference Between
Emotions and Feelings," *Psychology Today*, February 23, 2022,
https://www.psychologytoday.com/us/blog/the-pleasure-
is-all-yours/202202/the-important-difference-between
-emotions-and-feelings#:~:text=Despite%20the%20words
%20being%20used%20interchangeably%2C%20
emotions%20and,emotions%20but%20are%20generated%20
from%20our%20mental%20thoughts.

2. Angela Haupt, "Why Is Everyone Working on Their Inner
Child?", reference to quote by Shari Botwin, April 6, 2023,
https://time.com/6268636/inner-child-work-healing/.

3. Laura A. Jana, "Changing Diapers," Ages & Stages page,
Healthy Children, last updated May 19, 2021, https://www.
healthychildren.org/English/ages-stages/baby/diapers-
clothing/Pages/Changing-Diapers.aspx.

4. Alexis Conason, "How to Survive a Narcissistic Mother,"
Psychology Today, April 30, 2018, https://www.psychology

today.com/intl/blog/eating-mindfully/201804/how-survive-narcissistic-mother.

5. Association for Psychological Science, Publications page, "How Mother-Child Separation Causes Neurobiological Vulnerability Into Adulthood" entry, June 20, 2018, https://www.psychologicalscience.org/publications/observer/obs online/how-mother-child-separation-causes-neurobiological-vulnerability-into-adulthood.html.

6. Steven Stosny, "The Struggle to Balance Our Two Minds," *Psychology Today*, October 18, 2014, https://www.psychologytoday.com/za/blog/anger-in-the-age-entitlement/201410/the-struggle-balance-our-two-minds.

7. Frank J. Sulloway, "Sibling-Order Effects," excerpt from *International Encyclopedia of the Social & Behavioral Science*, 2nd ed., 2015, https://www.sciencedirect.com/topics/social-sciences/birth-order.

Chapter 12

1. Deepak Chopra, "Chapter One: The Law of Pure Potentiality," in *The Seven Spiritual Laws of Success: A Practical Guide to the Fulfillment of Your Dreams* (California: Amber-Allen Publishing, 1994), online excerpt from the Washington Post, https://www.washingtonpost.com/wp-srv/style/longterm/books/chap1/sevenspirituallaws.htm.

Chapter 13

1. John Lennon Plastic Ono Band, "Give Peace a Chance," September 13, 1969, track 6 on Live *Peace in Toronto 1969*, Apple.

2. *Oxford Learner's Dictionary*, s.v. "confrontation (*n.*)," accessed April 10, 2024, https://www.oxfordlearnersdictionaries.com/us/definition/english/confrontation?q=confrontation.

3. Leila Badyari, "Is Your Fear of Confrontation Giving You Anxiety?", *Thrive Global*, August 16, 2018, https://community.thriveglobal.com/is-your-fear-of-confrontation-giving-you-anxiety/.

4. Jeff Garlin and Larry David, interview by Martin Miller, *The Paley Center for Media*, Jan 5, 2012, https://www.youtube.com/watch?v=_wOMgX2AS8.

5. Ronald Reagan, excerpt from "Commencement Address, Eureka College," *Reagan Foundation*, video, May 9, 1982, https://www.reaganfoundation.org/ronald-reagan/reagan-quotes-speeches/commencement-address-eureka-college/.

6. Ramani Durvasula, *Should I Stay or Should I Go: Surviving A Relationship with a Narcissist* (New York: Post Hill Press, 2015).

Chapter 14

1. Rob Lowe, *Stories I Only Tell My Friends: An Autobiography* (New York: St. Martin's, 2012), 84.

2. C. G. Jung, *Letters, Volume I*, ed. Gerhard Adler and Aniela Jaffé, trans. R. F. C. Hull, Bollingen Series XCV (New York: Princeton University Press, 1973), 33.

3. Albert Camus, "Hope and the Absurd in the Work of Franz Kafka," in *The Myth of Sisyphus*, trans. Justin O'Brien, 2nd ed. (New York: Vintage International, 1955), 124.

About the Author

Jerry Giordano is a contentment counselor dedicated to sharing his learned gifts of achieving awareness and happiness. Because his clients will know their 7 Words from the start, he is quickly able to isolate their issues and immediately focus on replacing their sabotaging story with newfound self-esteem, inner peace, and contentment.

For many years Jerry was an award-winning advertising copywriter/creative director in New York City, Chicago, Los Angeles, Austin, and Dallas. He has worked for many of the world's largest advertising agencies, including Ogilvy and J. Walter Thompson, and has also served as the in-house creative director for the National Football League. He helped propel powerhouse brands such as Duracell, Kraft Foods, Amex, the NFL, Maxwell House Coffee, Philip Morris Corporate, Fox Studios, Food & Wine

Magazine, International Paper, Hardees, the LA Philharmonic, and countless others.

Being a polymath with an unquenchable curiosity has led Jerry to become a keen observer of human behavior, which he credits for much of his success in advertising and as the author of *Your 7 Words to a Happier You*. Jerry was a co-producer of one of the first TEDx events, penned four screenplays, studied sketch comedy professionally at Second City in Chicago, and has performed sketch comedy in NYC and the main stage at the Comic Strip in LA. He collects old cameras and quotes, photographs manhole covers wherever he goes, and is obsessed with the JFK assassination, which he will gladly discuss who did it over scotch or coffee. Does a world-class Sly Stallone performing Hamlet impression. Meditates regularly. Originally from New Jersey, Jerry now lives in the moment.